One Another

One Another

Jim Phillips

BROADMAN PRESS
Nashville, Tennessee

© Copyright 1981 • Broadman Press

All rights reserved.

4256-45

ISBN: 0-8054-5645-7

Dewey Decimal Classification: 248.4

Subject headings: CHRISTIAN LIFE//CHURCH FELLOWSHIP

Library of Congress Catalog Card Number: 81-66560

Printed in the United States of America

To Beth,
my wife and best friend,
with whom "one anothering" is such a joy!

Acknowledgments

I wish to express indebtedness to Dr. Ray Stedman. His rich insights into the Word, shared in many wonderful books, gave impetus to this work. I am especially grateful to Dr. Jay Adams for reviewing the manuscript, for making several helpful suggestions, and for giving me encouragement to see this project through. His own writings have done much to shape my thinking. I also want to thank Diann Manley for her sweet spirit and her excellent ability shown in unscrambling the scribble and preparing this manuscript for publication.

Acknowledgments

Foreword

Most churches have reduced fellowship to mean cold drinks and cookies in the social hall. If you go on a picnic, that's fellowship. If you laugh, sing, slap backs, tell stories, that's fellowship. But is it? Of course, these things are fine and in some way they relate to fellowship, but there's nothing distinctively Christian about them.

What is biblical fellowship? The answer to that question is given in the "one another" statements in the Bible. More than fifty of these statements command, illustrate, and detail biblical fellowship. These statements can be divided into four categories: (1) supportive, (2) confrontive, (3) preventive, and (4) prohibitive. This present volume deals only with the supportive statements, the foundation. My prayer is that, as you make this study, you'll catch a fresh vision of what church was intended to be.

In Acts we see a close connection between the ministry of the Word and fellowship (Acts 2:42). But for hundreds and hundreds of years sacramentalism muzzled the Word while institutionalism choked fellowship. Fortunately, the Reformers recovered the importance of preaching. But to this day, fellowship has never been properly restored. Thankfully, those in the relational theology movement have enabled us to see what's missing. However, their heavy reliance on pop psychology has delayed recovery.

For too long we have treated fellowship as something which comes by osmosis or is a by-product of something else. Neither is true. It is often thought that after about three years a church begins to reflect the personality of its pastor. The church may be perceived as winsome, appealing, and even compelling. People will bask in it, absorb it, enjoy it, but it might be cosmetic. What's going on underneath, as events may later reveal, is often quite a different story. So we mustn't confuse the appearance of an institution, however attractive it may be, with true biblical fellowship.

Secondly, fellowship isn't a by-product. People keep saying that if we just serve the Lord and do what's right, the fellowship will take care of itself. But that's not true. Fellowship isn't dependent on a burst of inspiration, a divine zap, or the chance chemistry of personalities. Fellowship, like worship and ministry, is something you structure for.

Because fellowship isn't an option, it would be a mistake to position it as a weekday opportunity. Put it there and, in most cases, more than half of the church family has been eliminated. Most churches already have the ideal structure for fellowship—Sunday School. We've said the purpose of Sunday School is to teach the Bible. That's good as far as it goes. I submit that it has a higher purpose—to change character. In Sunday School we have the same literature, same teacher, same class, same time. If we add the concept "one anothering," we have something wonderfully New Testament. We will not be just getting the Word *out,* but getting it *in.*

Contents

1
Fellowship One with Another

A sham Christianity is very popular today. It looks good: moral, orthodox, polite, and friendly. I am worried that we may be part of this. Except for a thin Christian veneer (which disappears when life becomes irritating and difficult), this is the same life we lived before we received Christ. This mild, inoffensive, occasionally-willing-to-do-a-good-deed-kind of life passes for Christianity in thousands of churches today. But it is a far cry from the conviction and compassion of the first-century church. This sham Christianity is widely accepted by the public, and not often condemned by the church. Because it is so prevalent today, we may think it is the real thing. But it's not. It's a fraud.

We will be examining what the Bible has to say about Christian fellowship. Many of the "one another" statements were given in the form of commands. We will study these statements so we can know better the kind of fellowship God wants us to have.

The first statement we will study is found in 1 John 1:7: "We have fellowship one with another." Can that be said of us? Do we have authentic, Christian fellowship with one another? Do we touch each other's lives in deep, significant ways? Unfortunately, this fellowship is often missing from our churches. One writer commented:

The neighborhood bar is possibly the best counterfeit there is to the fellowship Christ wants to give his Church. It's an imitation dispensing liquor instead of grace, escape rather than reality. But it is . . . an accepting . . . inclusive fellowship. . . . You can tell people secrets and they . . . don't tell others. . . . The bar flourishes not because

13

most people are alcholics, but because God has put into the human heart the desire to know and be known, (the desire) to love and be loved. And so many seek the counterfeit (of God's fellowship) at the price of a few beers.[1]

Sad, isn't it? The genius of the church is the unique fellowship it can have in Jesus Christ. People want and need this fellowship. But in so many instances the church simply doesn't offer it.

I read of one man who happened by a bookstore one day. Seeing a book inside entitled *How to Hug,* he went inside and bought it. When he got home he discovered the book wasn't what he thought it was. Instead of a warm, personal book on hugging, what he had actually purchased was an encyclopedia covering the alphabetized topics beginning with *how* and ending with *hug.* When I read that story, I wondered: *Could it be that our church perpetrates a similar disappointment? On the surface, we seem to be offering a warm, personal, and gratifying experience. But, in fact, very often that's not what people get.*

What is Christian fellowship? Many people equate friendliness with fellowship. But Christian fellowship is more than a casual greeting, the sharing of a joke or two, a brief observation about the morning lesson, and a momentary prayer for the sick and lost. Christian fellowship has three dependent components: (1) the sharing of our inner lives; (2) in the context of God's Word; and (3) in the energy of the Holy Spirit. Let's consider each component in turn.

The Sharing of the Inner Life

When a man is about to die, he speaks only of those things which are of the utmost importance. Shortly before Jesus died, he spoke words which are absolutely astounding in their implications. Jesus prayed "that they [you and I] all may be one; as thou, Father, art in me, and I in thee, that they also may be one in us" (John 17:21). Jesus said that we can enjoy the same fellowship with each other that he enjoyed with the Father. Who would think that we earthlings are capable of such oneness? Notice that Jesus said I *in* thee, not I *with* thee. This is the closest kind of intimacy. How is this intimacy achieved? We achieve it with one another in the same way Jesus achieved it with the Father: by opening up, by sharing our inner lives, by risking a transparency of soul.

I don't believe that the beauty of Jesus' earthly life can be understood apart from his remarkable intimacy with the Father. Many times Jesus left everybody and everything in order to be alone. For prolonged periods of time (out in the wilderness, in the middle of the night), Jesus opened his heart to the Father and the two communed. Did you know that the power and passion of Jesus' earthly life was singularly determined by those rendezvous with the Father?

In his high priestly prayer, Jesus said that we believers can enjoy this same kind of fellowship if we open up to each other, seek communion, and share our inner lives. In fact, this sharing of the inner life with fellow believers was so important to Jesus that he gave it top priority in his ministry. The Scriptures tell us that Jesus chose the twelve to be "with him." Day in and day out, week after week, month after month, these men became a close-knit fellowship. Jesus taught, trained, and encouraged the twelve. He reproved, rebuked, and admonished them. But, best of all, he loved them!

In effect, Jesus staked everything on the twelve. According to one old tradition, the angels became most upset with Jesus for doing this. "How foolish!" the angels scolded, when Jesus ascended to the Father. "No books, no schools, no massive organizations—just the twelve?" But, as it turned out, Jesus was right. The apostles steadied and nurtured God's infant church, guiding its growth from land to land. Were we to compare Jesus' two ministries—his public with his private—we would quickly see that it was his private ministry, his ministry with the twelve, that really paid off. His public ministry became less and less successful. But his ministry with the twelve provided the nucleus for God's great church.

The one distinctive of the Christian church is the new life found only in Jesus. If a church simply has the old life wrapped in pious language, it has absolutely no incentive to proclaim anything. The principle is simple: We can't give what we don't have. Conversely, we can't keep what we do have. If this new life ever takes hold, there will be a contagion about it which will cause the church to grow and grow.

This is clearly seen in the book of Acts. The early church enjoyed a daily fellowship (Acts 2:46). The very next verse states that the early church enjoyed a newfound favor with all the people (Acts 2:47). These two facts are related. The reality of God's new life was cultivated to such a degree in daily fellowship that the outside world couldn't help but marvel at the believers.

What a contrast existed between the church and the world! The church began in a violent, brutal, hostile society. First-century society was so violent that a master could kill his slave at whim and a parent could abandon his child to the gatekeeper, the gutter, or the garbage. Citizens, having nothing better to do, could go to the amphitheater and watch slaves murdered by the thousands. The cultured elite sat in the stands and howled in delight as men and beasts tore each other apart. In fact, one historian recorded that any citizen who invented a new way to destroy life was richly rewarded. Jesus planted his church in a world fractured and torn by hatred and strife. The church was where people accepted one another, cared for one another, comforted one another, and served one another. It was a *koinonia* where the people really got to know one another, rough edges and all, as they jointly submitted their lives to the authority of Jesus' teachings.

Ephesians calls this "the fellowship of the mystery" (Eph. 3:9). And, indeed, this is a mystery. Somehow the gospel of Jesus can break down the age-old barriers which separate and divide. The hurts and hostilities melt away once we stand in the warmth of God's grace.

Ironically, though, many people resist what they so desperately need. Even Christians do this. Some psychologists are now saying that 70 percent of today's population suffers from chronic loneliness. Many people feel that no one really knows them well and they don't feel like they really know anyone else. Do you remember the poem, "No Man Is an Island"? The title of Donne's poem expresses a biblical truth: whether we know it or not, we need each other. "Be able to comprehend with all saints . . . the love of Christ" (Eph. 3:18). We can never know this love by ourselves; it is best experienced in fellowship *with the saints*. That's why Jesus said, "Where two or three are gathered together in my name, there am I in the midst of them" (Matt. 18:20). Jesus will not fully manifest himself to us unless we are engaged in a sincere and open fellowship with other believers. We may pray, study, serve, and give individually, but our experience with God will be incomplete unless we experience his Son in the lives of fellow believers.

Without a doubt the chief hindrance to Christian fellowship is the widespread practice of Christians pretending not to have any problems. Christians, putting on their everything-is-all-right masks, deliberately participate in a conspiracy of silence. We are intent on conveying to the world that we have no problems of any real consequence. This supersaint image—everything is under control, everything is just fine—is nothing new.

When Moses came down from Mount Sinai, he didn't know why the people were shielding their faces. But it didn't take him long to figure it out. Apparently his face was all aglow. Moses decided to cover his face with a veil, a perfectly proper action in view of the circumstances. But, in time, Moses came to know something that the children of Israel didn't know. As time passed, the brightness faded to nothing more than a dim glow; but Moses wore his veil anyway. Why? Because he was afraid—afraid that his people would interpret his fading glory as a sign of his fading glory. (2 Cor. 3:13).

We hide behind veils today. We don't want anyone to see our fading glory, so we project an everything-is-fine image to the world. Some call it being shy and reticent, but it is just a veil covering up faded glory. When the Bible says, "Confess your faults one to another, and pray for one another, that ye may be healed" (Jas. 5:16), it is assuming that we have faults, that we need prayer, and that we need healing. Sometimes our veils of pride communicate to others that we think we have no faults, that we need no prayers, and that we need no healing. The Bible instructs church members to encourage, to forgive, to bear one another's burdens, and to be tender-hearted. When we act as if we have no problems, we cannot experience the loving care fellow church members can give.

If we would just risk vulnerability, we would see that other Christians are also struggling. Dr. Ray Stedman, pastor of the Peninsula Bible Church in Palo Alto, California, read 1 Corinthians 6:9-10 to his congregation one day.

Know ye not that the unrighteous shall not inherit the Kingdom of God? Be not deceived: neither fornicators, nor idolators, nor adulterers, nor effeminate, nor abusers of themselves with mankind, nor thieves, nor covetous, nor drunkards, nor revilers, nor extortioners, shall inherit the kingdom of God.

On the spur of the moment, Dr. Stedman asked the people in his congregation to raise their hands if they had problems with any of those sins. A forest of hands shot up. A young person, visiting the services that day, was very much surprised. Later he remarked, "Boy, those are my kind of people." If we share our burdens, we'll find believers who identify with us—people who are *our* kind of people.

In addition to finding people in the church with problems like ours, we can find help. The gospel has answers to our problems. Believers who have successfully applied God's Word to their problems would like to help others do the same. Just to know that other believers love us, care for us, pray for us, and extend themselves to us is a marvelous blessing. It is unique to Christian fellowship.

Christian fellowship involves sharing our inner lives—our thoughts and feelings, our strengths, and weaknesses. However, that's not all of it.

In the Context of God's Word

The second component of Christian fellowship is immensely important. Non-Christians can get together and share their innermost thoughts. There's nothing distinctively Christian about that. But once the non-Christian shares his innermost thought—what next? Where does he go from there? How does he put his life back together? Many schools of psychology are competing for his attention. Which one should he choose? The Christian, however, doesn't have to choose from different schools within the realm of human genius. The Christian finds his answers in God's Word, which is resonant in its authority because it is divinely inspired and incapable of error. Fellowship, if it is to be Christian, must be conducted in the context of God's Word.

Unfortunately, many Christians have attempted to share themselves *apart* from God's Word. A meeting begins with a Scripture reading that only serves as a springboard for testimony time. Instead of engaging God's Word and making specific application to day-to-day life, these Christians meet simply to tell what God has done for them. Now that's fine for a meeting or two, but it has its limitations. When the focus is on the past instead of the present, on victories instead of failures, on self instead of God, a staleness settles in. Perhaps some well-meaning Christians will then try to overcome the staleness by embellishing their testimonies. Call it "selective truth-telling" if you want to, but I sometimes believe that more lies are told during testimony time than at any other time.

The basis of Christian fellowship reinforces this principle of sharing within the context of God's Word: "That which we have seen and heard declare we unto you, that you also may have fellowship with us: and truly our fellowship is with the Father and with his Son, Jesus Christ" (1 John 1:3).

First, we should notice that the gospel—"that which we have seen and heard"—is the basis of true Christian fellowship. John's testimony to non-Christians could be stated like this: We want you to know the same God we know. We want you to know the same salvation we know. For only in this way can we have common ground for fellowship. The Greek word for *fellowship, koinonia,* means communion or the sharing of a common experience. Accepting the gospel of Jesus Christ is absolutely indispensable to Christian fellowship. There *must* be a common participation in the grace of God, in the salvation of Christ, and in the blessings of the Holy Spirit. If not, there can be no fellowship.

Christian fellowship involves a clean break from the old life. The Scriptures say: "Have no fellowship with the unfruitful works of darkness" (Eph. 5:11). "For what fellowship hath righteousness with unrighteousness? and what communion hath light with darkness?" (2 Cor. 6:14b). "Be ye not equally yoked" (2 Cor. 6:14a). "Come out from among them, and be ye separate" (2 Cor. 6:17). Clearly, Christian fellowship is fiercely dedicated to uprooting all of the old life. Or, to put it positively, Christian fellowship will settle for nothing less than the new life. "If we walk in the light, as he is in the light, we have fellowship one with another" (1 John 1:7). Walking where God walks, living like Jesus lived is the *condition* of Christian fellowship. But if we do not walk in the light, if this new life does not emerge, there's no fellowship. Christian fellowship requires the gospel and the new life which only the gospel can produce. Acts 2:42 helps us catch a glimpse of what true fellowship is like. The church, with more than three thousand members, "continued stedfastly in the apostles' doctrine and fellowship, and in breaking of bread, and in prayers." The apostles' doctrine constituted much of what we now call the New Testament.

Jesus promised them that he would help them remember "all things." Under the scrutiny of this collective remembrance, our New Testament was authored. The early church focused on doctrine, that is, on the Bible, the Word of God.

Notice the linkage between the Word and fellowship. Fellowship must be in the context of God's Word. In an atmosphere of warmth and support, we should allow fellow believers to help us apply the principles of God's Word to our lives. All of our lives—our thinking, our acting, and our reacting—is to be reshaped according to the principles of God's Word.

There must be this kind of sharing. We must find those believers with whom we can share and be nurtured in the Word. It's impossible to relate to everybody in a church of any size. God desires that we cultivate close relationships with a smaller circle of Christians than the entire membership. We need this fellowship because without it we will lack accountability to the truth. If there's no accountability to the fellow believers, then there's no accountability to the truth. That being the case, all kinds of self-deception can settle in, causing our lives not to be testimonies to much. We need fellow believers, but that's not enough. The written Word, the Bible, must be what draws us together. The Scriptures advocate that we "be perfectly joined together." How? "In the same mind and in the same judgment" (1 Cor. 1:10). However, there's a third component to Christian fellowship.

In the Energy of the Holy Spirit

Why do we need the Spirit? Because his ministry is crucial to biblical fellowship. For example, we need the Holy Spirit to help us select those Christians with whom we're to become close. We need the Spirit to help us discern who we really are, to learn what the Word is saying, and to structure a specific how-to strategy from the Word. Additionally, we need the Spirit to help us obey what we've learned and then to help others to do the same. We also need the know-how to share biblical insights in meaningful ways—when to be firm, when to be gentle, when to support, and when to confront. The Spirit gets us out of the "flesh" (our natural way of thinking and doing) and into the "Spirit" (God's way of thinking and doing). There's just no way our fellowship can be Christian unless the Spirit himself is energizing the whole process.

In his book, *The Church Before the Watching World,* Francis Schaeffer contends that the church must exhibit both a visible holiness and a visible love. But, without the Holy Spirit, Schaeffer writes, there will either be a holiness without love (legalism) or a love without holiness (sentimentalism). Of course, the world is turned off by both legalism and sentimentalism. If ever the church, in the power of the Holy Spirit, comes to exhibit love and holiness, the world will really take notice and conclude that Christians have been with Jesus (Acts 4:13). Church just isn't church unless there's fellowship: the sharing of the inner life, in the context of the Word, and in the energy of the Spirit.

2
Accept One Another

God wants in his church a fellowship so amazing, so utterly beyond human capacity, that even the angels will marvel. Paul talked about "the fellowship of the mystery" (Eph. 3:9), saying all men are to see it. But verse 10 speaks of something else: "That through the church the manifold wisdom of God might now be made known to the principalities and powers in the heavenly places" (RSV). Now who are these principalities and powers? Angels! It's as though believers are on stage and the angels in the audience. Our script, the Word of God, tells us exactly what to do. When we do it, the angels learn something wonderful. Arthur Custance said:

I believe . . . that God wishes to show forth that aspect of His being which the angels have never comprehended, namely His love, without at the same time surrendering that part of His being which they do understand, namely His holiness.[2]

Love and holiness are the two essential ingredients of a Christ-centered fellowship. How do we bring this about? How do we cultivate a fellowship for all men to see, a fellowship worthy of the angel's study? The answer, of course, comes from the Word of God. As you reflect on the "one another" statements, you may say, "It's all so clear! Why haven't I seen this before? It's so black and white! How did my church miss it?" I don't know, but I'm convinced that unless these "one another" statements are activated, the church isn't church. It's a skeleton without a body!

The supportive "one another" statements are positive and foundational. Romans 15:7 is such a statement: "Accept one another, then, just as Christ accepted you, in order to bring praise to God" (NIV). This verse can very logically be divided into four answers to the questions, What? Who? How? and Why?

What?

What are we to do? We are to offer acceptance. This is one of the most affirming things we can do. Surprisingly, though, many people don't feel accepted by anybody. Being left out, shunned, or neglected is not a very good feeling. If we experience rejection often enough, we begin to question our own self-worth. When that happens, we start locking other people out of our lives and locking ourselves in. God doesn't want that. God wants us to experience all of the joys of deep Christian fellowship. That's why he gave this command to accept one another.

Who?

This command is addressed to "one another"—to believers. As mentioned in chapter 1, receiving the gospel is absolutely essential to being part of a Christian fellowship (1 John 1:3). Putting this negatively, Proverbs 18:5 says: "It is not good to accept the person of the wicked." Of course, this doesn't mean we're to distance ourselves from an unbeliever. But it does mean that no unbeliever can share completely in our fellowship until he has accepted Jesus as his Lord. Now, shocking as this may be, we may be talking about church members.

In Jeremiah 14:9 we read, "We are called by thy name." Verse 10 says, "The Lord doth not accept them." Apparently some numbered among God's people were not acceptable to him. In effect, were they living in our day, they'd be on the church roll. Verse 10 says, "Thus have they loved to wander." In other words, they departed from the straight and narrow to do their own thing—and enjoyed it! In verse 7, they admitted, "Our backslidings are many; we have sinned against thee." Verse 10 says, "They have not refrained their feet." Their pattern was in and out, no stedfastness; they just couldn't be counted on!

Now, sad to say, there are people today on church rolls who fit this profile. They answer to the name Christian but the bottom line is they don't live what they profess. There is always this pattern of way-ward wandering! If whim and mood happen to agree, they may be there, but don't count on it. And so it is, because they're always backsliding, God will one day say, "This is not acceptable with me." Isn't that sobering? Remember, though, the acceptance of Christian fellowship is intended for only true believers.

How?

How are we to offer this acceptance? Romans 15:7 says to do it "just as Christ accepted you." How did he accept us? He accepted us just as we were. "While we were yet sinners, Christ died for us" (Rom. 5:8). In other words, though we were ugly, Jesus made a real sacrifice to reach out to us. That's what we're to do. We're not to wait until others conform to our expectations. God didn't do that to us, and we're not to do it to others. Instead, we're to go out of our way, reaching out, even if it costs us something.

It's important that we see the *basis* of Christian acceptance. Galatians 2:6 says, "God accepteth no man's person." You see no one, absolutely no one, is accepted by God on the basis of merit. We all come to God in precisely the same way: "By grace are ye saved through faith; and that not of yourselves: it is the gift of God: not of works, lest any man should boast" (Eph. 2:8-9). Acceptance is a gift, a gift of grace. We've known that at least in terms of our own rela-tionship with God. But what about our relationships with others? Unfortunately, too many Christians refuse to let grace be the basis of their acceptance of others. Instead, when it comes to making friends, works becomes the criteria. Some Christians accept only those peo-ple to whom they are already attracted—people who like what they like and do what they do. The world offers acceptance on that basis, but the church is supposed to be different. We're to accept people on the basis of grace.

Let's say that there's somebody in my church I really don't like. I may have some very understandable reasons for not liking him. Or perhaps, as I've observed this person from a distance, something about him repels me. So I decide to keep my distance. Of course I'll be polite and cordial. But in no real way will I offer acceptance. In making that decision, what have I done? I've set up a standard (which Christ never did to me), and I've decided to reject or accept people according to how they measure up to my standard.

Through the years, the Christian community has used various standards (ranging from silly to sinful) to determine who is acceptable. Three of them are riches, race, and religion.

Unfortunately, money talks—even in the church. There's absolutely no biblical reason for church members to give preferential treatment to the rich. But, very often it happens. Even the early church fell into this trap, causing James to write, "You are breaking this law of our Lord's when you favor the rich and fawn over them; it is sin" (Jas. 2:9, TLB). The problem is not that rich people can't be God's children too—they can! But, as James wrote, "Judging a man by his wealth shows that you [we] are guided by wrong motives" (Jas. 2:4, TLB). Romans 12:16 goes even further when it says that we're to relate to people of "low estate." We're to make it a point to establish meaningful contact with the poor and powerless.

Do we do that? Not very well. Most churches exhibit the principle "like attracts like." There are rich-people churches, poor-people churches, and middle-class churches. To be fair, so very often, it's not that the rich don't want to be with the poor; it may be that the poor don't want to be with anybody. That's why the poor tend not to join any institution, including the church. How Christ-honoring it would be, though, if certain members of the church were led of the Lord to be a blessing to these people, giving not only their money but also giving themselves! Not much of this is happening, I'm afraid. Instead, in very subtle, almost unconscious ways, we accept or reject people according to the standard of riches.

A second standard used, more decisive and more destructive than the first, is race. Do you realize that the church is vulnerable to the charge of being "out Christianized" by the sports world? Evangelist Billy Graham says, "We have let the sports world, the entertainment world, the military, industry, and education outstrip us" as far as race relations is concerned. It is a well-known fact that the most segregated hour in the week is the eleven o'clock worship hour. Christians have mocked God's Word by accepting or rejecting people on the basis of race.

Jesus said that we're to love others *as he loved us*. Why did he love us? Because of the color of our skin? No. He loved us, not because of our race, but because of grace. Many churches show how little they understand grace when they refuse to love redemptively those other races.

A third standard used to accept or reject people is religion. By religion, I'm thinking of the conflict between liberals on the one side and legalists on the other. A legalist has been defined as someone who lives in mortal terror that someone somewhere is having a good time. They seem to equate religion with a long list of rules, not biblical rules, just the invention of a certain narrow life-style. If someone doesn't measure up, they reject him.

Have you ever known a church which turns out a lot of carbon copies of the preacher? Some churches exert tremendous pressure and at times can be downright hostile to anyone who doesn't conform. But if the dynamics of good and evil are examined, it is obvious that good is rich in its variety, while evil is monotonously the same. So, whenever a church turns out one product, whenever there's much conformity, beware! Legalism is at work.

The legalist seems to be more faithful than the rest. Not because of what he does but because of what he *doesn't* do. However, surprisingly, in Romans 14, Paul said the religious legalist was "weak in faith." Why? Because he focuses on works more than grace, the negative more than the positive, on what he should do instead of on what God has done. Romans 14:1 says, "Accept him whose faith is weak" (NIV). That is, recognize your common heritage in the Lord. True, he may think differently on some issues, but don't argue. Remember, the legalist has been accepted where he is by Christ, just as we have been accepted where we are.

The command to accept one another is foundational to church life. It represents the very first step upon which God builds his church: our acceptance of salvation and God's acceptance of us. We need to follow God's example of accepting us when we select our friends. Usually we choose our friends on the basis of merit, not on the basis of grace.

How can we enter into relationships on the basis of grace? Simple. First of all, pray. Jesus prayed all night before he entered into a relationship with the twelve. Jesus didn't choose the twelve nicest men. Instead, alert to the Father's guidance, Jesus chose some men who weren't all that nice or, for that matter, all that competent.

Building relationships on grace means accepting anyone the Father accepts. In faith, we enter into the relationship that God has chosen whether we feel like it or not.

Of course, God knows this isn't always easy. Some people can be exasperating. They have an uncanny ability to drive us to our limits, but not to God's limit. Paul wrote, "May the God who gives endurance and encouragement give you a spirit of unity among yourselves" (Rom. 15:5, NIV). Since today's church hasn't always enjoyed such unity, let's see if we can find some clues that will help.

Paul said that God gives endurance. According to verse 5, there's absolutely no reason for believers to break relationship (either by declaration or by an unannounced parting of the ways) because God will give the capacity to endure. Just because we are Christians doesn't mean everyone is going to like us. The truth is we all live in contradiction. Our old nature emerges from time to time, causing us to be miserably ugly. God knows that we will have this struggle. He knows that some Christians, so thoroughly entrenched in old ways, will give others a hard time. So he puts at our disposal this amazing capacity to endure. Biblical endurance is much more than putting up with someone. Its goal is "a spirit of unity" (Rom. 15:5). No matter how exasperating another believer may be, we are neither to retaliate nor give up. Instead, we are to go out of our way to be blessings to this person.

That sounds good, but we are human. We can't exercise that kind of endurance, but the Scriptures say *God* can. The capacity to endure comes from him. No matter how obnoxious another believer may be, God can empower us to participate redemptively in that person's life. If we have never experienced this capacity to endure, it could be that we've never asked for it. "Ye have not," James said, "because ye ask not" (4:2). Chances are we haven't thought to ask God for endurance when we have been wronged. Instead, we do what comes naturally; and as a result, many relationships have ended. Perhaps right now you're conscious of a relationship in bad repair. Ask God to give you his endurance. He'll do it. A patience and power greater than any you've ever known before will enable you to reestablish that relationship.

Hebrews 12:3 says, "Consider him that endured . . . lest ye be wearied and faint in your own minds." In other words, if we think we've got it rough, we need to consider what Jesus went through. We haven't had to shed our blood, have we? Let's face it, you and I scarcely know what it is to endure. But because Jesus endured so much for us, we're to endure with one another.

Notice the way endurance is linked with encouragement. Romans 15:5 says that God gives both. Isn't it true that we tend to give up when we become discouraged? We think that person is never going to change. But the God who gives endurance will also give encouragement. Not a false optimism, but, in the words of Romans 15:4, "the encouragement of the Scriptures" (NIV). What does that mean? Just this: If we will just take time to read what the Scriptures have to say, we will see their marvelous provisions for all problems. No matter what the problem, God has a solution. When this finally dawns on us, we have hope. We will feel encouraged, justifiably encouraged. This encouragement will enable us to endure.

There's really no justification for discouragement—at least not where another believer is involved. Such discouragement declares two things. It shows that we think this believer will never change (which may be right; given his own inclinations, he won't). It also declares a belief that God can never change him; and that, in the most serious way, undermines the power of grace. Remember, the basis of our acceptance is grace—divine, undeserved grace. So, in moments of irritation and moments of anguish, don't just focus on what a person has done. Focus, instead, on what the grace of God can do. This, more than anything else, is the difference between the way the world accepts people and the way we do.

"May the God who gives endurance [that is, the ability to participate redemptively in another person's life even when the natural you doesn't feel like it] and encouragement [that is, the ability to focus on what grace can do, not just on what so and so has done] give you a spirit of unity among yourselves as you follow Christ Jesus" (Rom. 15:5, NIV). Notice how this unity is achieved: "As you follow Christ Jesus." Picture a triangle. Let the apex of this triangle represent Jesus (for he is the Head of the church). Let one side of the triangle represent you, while letting the other side represent a fellow believer. The greatest difference between you and the other believer is at the base of the triangle. That's the way it is in the church. You and the other believer may not be very far along in the new life, so in many respects you're still far apart. But, as each follows the Lord, like the sides of that triangle, you will come closer and closer together. That's what Paul meant. It is *only* as believers come closer to the Lord Jesus that we come closer to each other.

Why?

Why are we to accept one another? In the words of Romans 15:7, we're to do it "in order to bring praise to God" (NIV). If ever the world sees a church accepting people on the basis of grace, the world is going to know that God is at work. How will it know? Because that is the only deduction it can make. Our world knows the human spirit well enough to know that the natural self doesn't accept people on the basis of grace. There may be enough goodness in the natural self to make an occasional gesture of kindness. But it goes completely against our nature to keep on extending ourselves to a person who does not respond positively.

Only God can keep us sufficiently determined in our love that, when ingratitude greets us, we can still be his channels of blessing. Only God can give the wisdom which knows how to love the sinner, while at the same time uprooting the sin. Only God can give us faith which focuses not on who a person is but on whom he can become. If and when a church accepts people on the basis of grace, the world will really take notice. Our blundering, blinded world may confuse a lot of things, but it won't confuse this. People will know right away God is responsible.

Do you want to praise God? There's no better way to do it than to obey the scriptural injunction, "Accept one another." The world may admire good preaching, good singing, good programs, and all the rest. But what will really capture the world's interest is a community of people who believe in grace, not just as a principle of salvation but as a principle of relating to one another in the body. If we really want to praise God, if we really want to win the lost, Romans 15:5,7 challenges us to live by grace. When we Christians live this way, the world's going to be wanting what we have!

3
Bear with One Another

Have you ever heard the saying: "I love mankind—it's people I can't stand"? The human spirit has an amazing ability to compartmentalize. When we think about humanity, we're fond of saying how we love our fellow human beings and how we're willing to do anything to help them. But when we think about certain people we know, suddenly our undying love dies; all of our good intentions go right out the window. This is how it is when it comes to fellowship. Fellowship sounds good in the abstract; but when it gets down to specifics, our lofty ideals are put to the test and very often we, not they, fail. As has been said:

> To dwell above with saints we love,
> Oh, that will be glory
> But to live below with saints we know
> Well, that's another story![3]

Fortunately, God realizes that it's much easier to perceive than to achieve Christian fellowship. That's why he gave us specific instructions on how to relate to fellow Christians even though they, like we, are far from perfect. One instruction is passive in nature; the other, more active.

Bear with One Another

I therefore, the prisoner of the Lord, beseech you that ye walk worthy of the vocation wherewith ye are called, with all lowliness and meekness, with longsuffering, forbearing one another in love; endeavouring to keep the unity of the Spirit in the bond of peace (Eph. 4:1-3).

We'll look at this text in its entirety, but particularly notice this phrase: "forbearing one another in love." *The Living Bible* translates this to mean "making allowance." The *Amplified* version says that we're to "bear with" one another. To clarify, let me point out what this phrase doesn't mean. To "bear with" somebody, "making allowances," doesn't mean that we simply tolerate others, greeting them with a rehearsed politeness. Nor does it mean that we overlook all of their shortcomings, chalking them up to human frailty.

Bearing with somebody really means that, once a sin has been acknowledged and a strategy for overcoming it begun, we'll back off and give our fellow Christian a chance. We'll not pounce on his first slipup with warnings and scowls. Instead, we will realize that he didn't fall into this sin pattern overnight and that he's not going to get out of it overnight. So with confidence that God is going to give him victory, we will bear with him. That is, we'll stay close enough to give support but far enough away to allow for freedom, and maybe even mistakes.

Bearing with one another is no easy task—especially when the failures are so needless. Even Jesus lamented, "O faithless and perverse generation, ... How long am I to bear with you?" (Matt. 17:17, RSV). If our Lord's patience were taxed by people, we can be sure that ours will be. What made these people perverse? It was their unwillingness to rely on the divine supply. How exasperating to bear with people and to know that all the resources for change are available, but no improvement is made. Nonetheless, the Scriptures declare that we're to bear with one another and tell us how we're to do it.

First, we're to do it with all *lowliness.* Another word for lowliness is *humility.* Humility means that not only are we aware of our many shortcomings but we are also aware of where our good qualities come from. They come from God. Lowliness relates to forbearance in two ways. We will be more able to bear with another believer's shortcomings if (1) we are tuned in to our own shortcomings, and (2) if we are turned on by God's ability to overcome them. Please notice the Bible says we are to exercise *all* lowliness. In other words, this ministry of bearing with other Christians requires a complete humility.

Second, we're told to bear with one another in *meekness.* Meekness isn't weakness. The Greek word for meekness, *prautes,* means to harness a wild animal. Meekness, then, means having our wills to be wild broken. Meekness means being submissive. It means being teachable. It means being moldable. How does meekness relate to forbearance? Because we are no longer our own (we are now in God's harness), we will not do what we might have otherwise done when another believer fails us. Instead, we will be God's person to this believer, sharing the truths we've learned, which will more than remedy the situation.

Third, we're told to bear with one another with *long-suffering.* Another word for long-suffering is patience. But the word long-suffering itself may give us the clue to understanding how patience relates to forbearance. We're to become so involved in this other believer's life that we hurt, really hurt, when this person is trapped in sin. Our commitment to Christ and hence to this fellow believer is to have such a quality about it that we'll be willing to suffer for a long, long time.

We're also told to bear with one another in *love.* In fact, the love chapter of the Bible, 1 Corinthians 13, teaches us that love "beareth all things" (v. 7). How is love able to do this? The answer, I think, is found in this very same verse.

Love "believeth all things." Does this mean that we're to be gullible? No, by "believeth all things" Paul meant that we are to believe that another person will achieve his best. One might say, "That sounds more than gullible—that sounds stupid." It may sound stupid, but it actually isn't. You see, to believe in someone doesn't mean to be optimistic about *his* ability to change. What we are to be optimistic about is *God's* ability to change him. Everyone acts according to the image he has. That means if we change his image, we change him! How do we change his image? By believing in him the way God does.

Have you ever known what it is to have somebody believe in you? I have. I'll always be grateful to my eleventh-grade English teacher because she believed in me when I didn't believe in myself. I was an easily unnoticed student in a huge high school. But for some reason this English teacher took an interest in me. Before long I exchanged my belief about me for hers because I liked hers better. This experience taught me an indelible lesson . . . scarcely anything is more creative than one person believing in another. Few Christians do it, but it's one of the most powerful things we can do. For our beliefs will change that person, diminishing the time and the anguish of our forbearance.

The love chapter also says love "hopeth all things." This doesn't mean merely a casual wish—a God-give-me-everything-I-want prayer. In a more intense way, motivated by love and moved by the Spirit, we're to catch a vision of who this person could become. By catching a vision, I don't mean receiving a message in a trancelike state. Since the Bible tells us what God can do in the human heart, our vision is to come from the Word.

Of course, in situations like this, we are painfully aware that there is a big difference between what God says he will do and what our friends are now doing. This difference between the *is* and the *ought* constitutes the vision zone. So, we are to prayerfully get it into our minds who this person could really become. Allow God to first correct and then to empower your vision. And, then, once assured that your vision is from God, share it with your friend with expectation and hope. Articulate the vision—spell it out, hold it up, and let the vision work. Can't you envision how this kind of hope will energize your ministry of forbearance?

Lastly, we're told that love "endureth all things." This means that we're willing to go through a lot to preserve the relationship. Ephesians 4:3 says that we're to endeavor "to keep the unity of the Spirit in the bond of peace." *Endeavor* literally means to be zealous, to be diligent. That means we're to do everything we can to keep that unity. Very interestingly, in verse one Paul identified himself as a "prisoner of the Lord." Paul didn't say he was a prisoner of a Herod or of Nero but—get this—a prisoner of the Lord! Paul used the same root word for *prisoner* when he wrote about the "bond" of peace. Isn't that great? Instead of a prisoner of war, a Christian is to be a prisoner of peace. To be prisoners of peace means willfully to lock ourselves into an ironclad resolve to keep the Spirit's unity. With lowliness, meekness, long-suffering, and love, we're to do everything we can to bear with one another.

Bear One Another's Burdens

Our second biblical instruction is found in Galatians 6:2: "Bear ye one another's burdens." This passage may sound like the Ephesians passage ("bear with one another"), but there's a difference. The Ephesians passage is more passive in nature in that we are told not to intrude too much (lowliness), but to be meek and patient, giving God's love time to work. The Galatians passage calls for a more active participation. We're to help fellow believers to bear their burdens.

Of course, this raises the question: What is a burden? Is it material in nature? Physical in nature? Spiritual in nature? Is it the same thing as Paul's thorn or Jesus' cross? Although the Greek word for burden *(baros)* can refer to something which is material (1 Thess. 2:6) or physical (Matt. 20:12), the context of Galatians 6 makes it abundantly clear that it's a *spiritual* burden which is in view. In Galatians Paul systematically listed spiritual qualities, both good and evil (ch. 5). In Galatians 6:1 Paul used the word "spiritual" when he gave his instruction to restore those overtaken in a fault. So the burden-bearing ministry has to do with spiritual burdens.

What is the difference between a thorn, a burden, and a cross? A thorn is a *preventive* to sin, a burden is a *consequence* of sin, and a cross is an *alternative* to sin. Let me explain. Paul talked about his "thorn in the flesh." We don't know what this thorn was, but we do know its purpose: "Lest I should be exalted above measure" (2 Cor. 12:7). In Paul's own words, then, the thorn was given to save him from pride. Now, a burden is anything that contributes to sin. Whatever it is that threatens to separate the saint from self, society, or the Savior is a burden. Simply put, a burden is spiritual oppression.

A cross is an instrument of death. To bear a cross, then, means that you are giving up—not your cigarettes, your boat, some other luxury, or habit—no, you are giving up *you!* A cross means the renunciation of the old life (Gal. 6:14; Phil. 3:18,19) and an acceptance of the new (Luke 14:27). So these three terms—a thorn, a burden, and a cross—don't belong in the same category because their meanings are quite different.

What we're focusing on here is a burden—that which causes spiritual oppression. Are we to handle these burdens by ourselves? Most people do and, sadly, even most Christians do. Some of these Christians justify their refusal to open up by pointing to Paul's words in Galatians 6:5, "For every man shall bear his own burden." Apparently, their principle of operation is, *This is a private matter between me and God. I'll work this out on my own.*

However, the burden Paul talked about in Galatians 6:5 is quite different from the burden in Galatians 6:2. In fact, an entirely different word is used *(phortion,* not *baros).* The burden Paul wrote about in Galatians 6:5 is not the burden of sin, but the burden of ministry. Every believer is to have a ministry because, among other things, this ministry will be a part of God's solution to the ministering believer's sin problem. There is to be a reciprocal relationship between being and doing, between the gifts and the fruit, between fellowship and ministry.

However, in Galatians 6:2 Paul focused on *being* and the fellowship which will produce the fruit. That's vital because who we are is more important to God than what we can do. On the other hand, it is extremely urgent for us to work out what God works in.

Galatians 6:2 means exactly what it says: *every* believer is to help bear other believers' burdens. Not every believer is to help restore one overtaken in a fault. For the Scripture is clear: only those who are "spiritual" (Gal. 6:1) are to do that. The ministry of restoring a stumbling believer is extremely delicate. It requires deep sensitivity and great spiritual depth. Tremendous harm can be done if immature Christians attempt this ministry. Harm can be done because usually immature Christians don't have the truths they need to have and often they don't have the proper motives.

Many churches have suffered needlessly because they haven't understood this principle. Only those mature in the faith should attempt the spiritual surgery of restoring a believer overtaken by sin. But once the believer has acknowledged his sin and has committed himself to the process of overcoming it, *then* other believers can join in and provide much-needed support.

Is this happening in our churches? Not really. We focus on material needs (money, food, clothing) and physical needs (illness or injury) but not on spiritual needs (our ongoing sin struggle). In most churches where there is a focus on spiritual needs, the focus is on the past ("what God did for me") and not the present ("what I now need for God to do in me"). There is, of course, a place for our victory testimonies because other Christians can be encouraged by what God has done in our lives. But victory testimonies—after the fact, after the time of crisis, after the battle has been won—are quite easy. By definition, at this stage in the process, there's no burden to bear. Much more difficult, but much more helpful, is sharing your struggle right when you're in the middle of it. Of course, pride causes us to resist sharing. But the burden-bearing ministry requires sharing because no one can bear with us what we don't share.

Put it down as incontrovertible fact— you and I and all other Christians must share our sin struggles if there's going to be a burden-bearing ministry. Certainly precautions must be taken. Expertise must be available. I'll speak to both of these concerns later. At this point let this truth put you under conviction: God wants every believer to share with total honesty the sin struggle he is presently engaged in. Why? Just to get out? Just to ventilate feelings? Just so you'll feel better? No, that's not the reason.

God wants us to experience the tremendous support we can receive when fellow believers become part of our answers. When this begins to happen, church will become something more than dry and formal ritual. It will be a place of deep friendships and lasting help. But if we don't share, then we will be trusting what God absolutely refused to trust: the desperately wicked heart. In one subtle way after another, our hearts will cause us to think that our spiritual condition is much better than it really is (Gal. 6:3; Rom. 12:3). As a result, we can drift in the dead sea of piety and pretense.

God knows what our hearts are like. Even after we walk the aisle in conversion or rededication (stating all of our best intentions) and even though we regularly attend, faithfully work, and generously support the work of the church, our inner lives can slip back into its old, cold condition. It's absolutely essential, then, for Christians to be in a regular fellowship where their lives are exposed to the light of God's Word. In Galatians 6:1, we see the ministry of restoration at work. But God does not stop there. We do, but God doesn't. God goes on to commend the ministry of burden-bearing for Christians. For saved, rededicated Christians still have, and always will have, sin problems. In fact, the more we conquer, the greater the battle. We mustn't ever underestimate what Satan will do. By our almost total neglect of the ministry of burden-bearing, we have shown how little we understand Satan's capacity and how little we understand God's provision.

If we were to begin a burden-bearing ministry in our churches, what would be involved? In general, the ministry of burden-bearing will involve confession (whenever a believer sins), comfort (whenever a believer hurts), encouragement (whenever a believer begins to lose hope), exhortation (whenever a believer needs a specific Word therapy), admonition (whenever a believer is heading for danger), and prayer.

In the words of 1 Thessalonians 5:17, we're to "pray without ceasing." That doesn't mean we're to drop the routines of day-to-day life. Hearts are to go out to fellow believers. We will lift them up to God in prayer with such intensity that even when we have finished praying, our prayers won't be finished with us. They will motivate our activities throughout the day. Imagine how rewarding it would be to have someone caring for you like that.

Are you beginning to see how this will work? There's no way to be in this kind of fellowship group and still drift in ho-hum ways. You'll either get better or worse (2 Cor. 2:16), but you won't remain the same. Everybody, I suspect, has had the experience of committing a certain sin over and over again. One of the reasons we're defeated is because we don't have fellow believers involved in our repenting process. You see, a small-group fellowship exerts a creative pressure on its members to conform to God's image. Would you like to go back to your group over and over again reporting failure? No, and since you couldn't fool them, your best alternative would be to give up the sin which has been defeating you.

One of the things I appreciate so much about God's fellowship design is not only are we *all* to be a part of it but also we're *all* to give and receive. It's not a matter of some people being the helpers and some being the ones helped. Every Christian is to function on *both* levels. This means that mature Christians are to receive counsel and that immature Christians are to give it. This is specifically pointed out in Galatians 6:6, "Let him that is taught in the word communicate unto him that teacheth in all good things." Admittedly, these verses in Galatians 6 are difficult to interpret. But, contrary to traditional interpretation, I'm not so sure that Paul is giving a commercial to pay the preacher. Paul urged a peership between the mature and the immature so that both can bless each other with the Word. God knows we're not perfect. However, our imperfections don't cancel out God's program for fellowship. To the contrary, it's precisely because we are as imperfect as we are that we need Christian fellowship—especially the ministry of burden-bearing.

The Bible clearly tells us what we are to bear. We are to bear temptation (1 Cor. 10:13). We are to bear "the milk of the Word" (1 Cor. 3:2). We are to bear exhortation (Heb. 13:22). We are to bear fruit (John 15:8). We are to bear God's name (Acts 9:15). We are to bear reproach (Heb. 13:13; 1 Pet. 4:14). And we're to bear our crosses (Luke 14:27).

Does that sound like an awful lot? It is. But remember what Jesus had to bear. In fact, we wouldn't even be where we are had not Jesus borne the penalty of our sins (Heb. 9:28). So, motivated by what God has done and by what he still wants to do, "bear with one another in love" (Eph. 4:2). More than that, "bear one another's burdens" (Gal. 6:2).

4
Care for One Another

The 1975 edition of *The Baptist Hymnal* has a hymn entitled, "Do You Really Care?" I always feel uneasy when I sing this song because I know in many ways I don't really care. I don't care the way I should.

Instead I've trained my eye not to see, cautioned my mind not to think about people within my circle of influence who are hurting. Jesus told a parable about men like me. They were religious men. But you know what they did? When they came on a man who was hurting, they passed by on the other side of the road. I do that.

I see those pictures of bony-faced little children—sick, hungry, staring their pathetic stare. But what do I do? Same thing, pass right by! So many unloved, unwanted people are wounded in spirit, wasting away. But to us they're only a faceless blur in the landscape of life. And so, with scarcely a halt in our step, we pass on by. To our shame, we prefer the other side of life with all its luxuries, gadgets, and modern-day conveniences. Caring, though, means stopping to take in what's going on and, if need be, going out of our way to meet the need.

The Bible says, "Care one for another" (1 Cor. 12:25). The command to care seems strange to some folk because to them caring is an emotion, so they wonder how God could command it. In the Greek, there are several different words for care. What is common to them all is the idea of giving thought, of showing interest, and of having a certain focus. Now, it's true that no one can command emotion, but God *can* tell us how to center our thoughts, how to

41

redirect our interest, and how to zero in on need. If you will, I want you to think about your brothers and sisters in the Lord. Do you know their needs? Maybe you ought to become more sensitive. Maybe you should ask God to show you what their needs are and then show you what you could do to help. Do you know the needs to be met in a ministry of caring?

The Needs to Be Met

One of the most beloved, power-packed parables Jesus ever told is the parable of the good Samaritan. It tells us not only what the needs are but also how to meet those needs. Some universal principles in this parable pretty well define what caring means.

"A certain man went down from Jerusalem to Jericho, and fell among thieves, which stripped him of his raiment, and wounded him, and departed, leaving him half dead" (Luke 10:30). In this one verse we learn of three needs. A man was robbed, wounded, and left half dead. Of course, all three of these needs are physical; but the Scriptures show these same things occurring in the realm of the spirit. Let's consider robbery. Ephesians talks about "the unsearchable riches of Christ" (3:8), the riches of his grace (1:7), mercy (2:4), and glory (3:16); indeed, of our whole spiritual inheritance (1:18). In Matthew 13, Jesus told how "the wicked one" will steal from you and me what God wants to give (v. 19). A possible interpretation of this parable could be that Satan would, if he could, steal everything. To be without clothes is to be exposed, humiliated, and unable to carry on. That's what Satan wants to do. He wants to ransack our souls to the extent that we'll be exposed, put to shame, and utterly deprived of what is needed to live.

However, not only was this Jericho-bound traveler robbed but he was also wounded. In the Greek, two words are used for wounded: *plege,* which means a blow, and *epitithemi,* which means to lay on. Literally, then, the robbers laid on the blows. Viciously and maliciously they beat this man senseless. The Scriptures tell us that this isn't the only kind of fighting going on. Ephesians 6:12 says, "We wrestle not against flesh and blood, but against principalities, and powers, . . . against spiritual wickedness in high places." The battle waged in our inner lives is far more devastating than any physical attack. For, as one proverb puts it: "A wounded spirit who can bear?" (Prov. 18:14). Ephesians says, "In time past . . . [we] were by nature the children of wrath" (2:3). That is, we had it within us, as unbelievers do today, to cause great harm to our inner selves. David's enemies caused him to cry: "My heart is wounded within me" (Ps. 109:22). Unless Jesus is our Lord, somewhere along the way we are going to line up with Satan and attack others, wounding within.

Robbed, wounded, and now the third crime those bandits committed. They left him "half dead." The term *half dead* is used nowhere else in the New Testament, but it is a marvelously descriptive term. Do you know people who are "half dead"? In Luke 15, the father greeted the prodigal with, "This my son was dead and is alive again." Deadness, then, may be related to leaving the Father; aliveness is coming back home. Many people today are dead. They are dead in that they are far from the Father. But they are still breathing, still existing, and still struggling to make sense of it all.

The tragedy is not just that people are in this condition, but that they've been left in this condition. Christians, though knowing the situation, pass right by. Luke tells us that the Levite saw the wounded man. According to the Greek, the Levite studied the situation with great intensity, carefully discerning exactly what was needed. He, more than anybody else, discerned the problem and recognized what to do, but he never lifted a finger to help.

Then a certain Samaritan came down the road and had compassion on the wounded man. The Samaritan bound up the man's wounds and "brought him to an inn, and took care of him." Before leaving the next day, the Samaritan gave the keeper of the inn some money and said, "Take care of him." Now, I interpret the inn to be the church and the keeper of the inn as representing pastoral leadership. Is that just my imagination? I don't think so. The same word used for "care" in this passage is used in 1 Timothy 3:5, "Take care of the church."

We often think of the first-century church as one bursting at the seams with spiritual people. But that may be too rosy of a picture. Remember, the apostle Paul lamented to the church at Philippi, "I have no man . . . who will . . . care for your state. For all seek their own, not the things which are Jesus Christ's" (Phil. 2:20-21). He was telling the people of this church that he was having a hard time finding a pastor who would really care for them. Paul was having a hard time because most of the pastors were worried about their own plans instead of God's plans. This is a real indictment. We ministers can be so tuned in to buildings, budgets, and baptisms that we don't provide the kind of pastoral care that God wants us to give. Unfortunately, we ministers have forgotten the instructions our Lord gave at the end of the parable of the good Samaritan, "Do thou likewise." What are we to do? Care for that person brought into the church, unhealed and hurting. "Take care of the church of God." Who? All of those people who have accepted Jesus as Lord.

Very briefly, let's see what this caring is to include.

How to Meet the Needs

In the first place, our caring is to help those who are robbed of the unsearchable riches of Christ. The first man in the parable "fell among thieves." Obviously, this man didn't know what was about to happen. He was caught by surprise. Point one: *Effective pastoral care will alert people to the way Satan operates.* Paul said of Satan, "We are not ignorant of his devices" (2 Cor. 2:11). Which is to say, we know his tricks, how he operates. Amazingly, though, many pastors and churches have reduced the whole concept of pastoral care to mean having a good bedside manner, to saying kind, sweet things to the sick and old. But it is precisely the carelessness of much pastoral care that allows so many to fall, not among thieves, but on the spiritual level to "fall into reproach and the snare of the devil" (1 Tim. 3:7). We must alert each other systematically to all of Satan's tricks so we won't be caught by surprise. The Bible says that this man was heading from Jerusalem to Jericho. Now, since Jerusalem was known as the city of God, could it be that this man was going in the wrong direction and that, as such, all of this could have been anticipated?

We're also told that the thieves stripped this man of his clothes. Point two: *Effective pastoral care will enable sin's victims to move past humiliation into a new dignity that can come only from God.* This is done by helping sin's victims to "put on the Lord Jesus Christ" (Rom. 13:14). We need to put on Jesus in whose image we were made. Clothes make us presentable. The only way we'll ever be presentable to God is to put on Jesus. Perhaps this notion of putting on Jesus seems a little strange to you. Ephesians 4:22 tells us to "put off . . . the old man." And conversely, Ephesians 4:24 tells us to "put on the new man." This new person is "created in righteousness and true holiness." To put on Jesus, then, is to put on holiness. But how? Are we only to exercise our will power and try to do better? No, we won't get very far if that's what we're doing. Notice that Romans 13:14 identifies Jesus as "Lord" and "Christ." Lordship has to do with power, authority, being in control. So, if Jesus is the Lord of life, he'll take control and give power needed to achieve his goodness. But what if we fall? The term "Christ" means the Messiah, the Deliverer. Jesus will pick us up and deliver us from our bondage. To help someone put on Christ, then, means to show them how to get a new image, how to become presentable to God, how to live in true righteousness and holiness.

As noted, the man on the Jericho road was wounded. Point three: *Effective pastoral care will teach people how to defend themselves against "the wiles of the devil."* Ephesians 6:11-18 gives a step-by-step account on how to do this. Each part of God's armor represents a specific strategy Christians are to use. It's very important to know that God's armor is to be put on just as God instructed. Do you know what these pieces of armor are? Truth, righteousness, the gospel of truth, faith, salvation, the Spirit, prayer, and supplication. Every Christian must be thoroughly familiar with his armor. So familiar, in fact, that he'll instinctively know what to do whenever he's under attack.

Luke 10:33 says, "As he [the good Samaritan] journeyed, came where he [the wounded traveler] was." Point four: *Effective pastoral care will be alert to the opportunities of ministry.* Many people go to their graves thinking that they had the love of God within them but that for some reason the opportunity to minister that love never came their way. But countless opportunities are before us. We need to be alert to them. If we don't care, we won't see. It's just that simple. Some Christians pray whenever they come upon hurt, wanting to know if God wants them to help. But, as Reinhold Niebuhr said: "The situation is the bearer of God's will." The very fact that there's suffering in your path means that you need to help. The good Samaritan didn't ask God what to do. He knew what to do. It's important for us to be alert and responsive to the suffering we find.

When the good Samaritan saw the wounded man, "he had compassion on him" (Luke 10:33). Point five: *Effective pastoral care will convey a genuine Christian warmth.* It's easy for people in the helping profession to become somewhat hard and callous. They see so much hurt that their defenses cause them to lose their compassion. The Greek word for *compassion* literally means to yearn deeply, to be moved from within. It's just not enough for us to give help in a cold, mechanical way. Equally important is the need for a genuine compassion to accompany our help.

Luke 10:34 tells us that after seeing the wounded man and having a compassion for him, the good Samaritan "went to him." Point six: *Effective pastoral care will minister to people where they are.* We mustn't insist that people come to church first or that they obtain a certain respectability or a certain knowledge before we can help. We're to begin right where they are. This means that we'll be with them, not just in a geographical sense, but in a personal sense. As best as we can, we're not only to listen to what they say but also we're to be sensitive to their feelings. Both feeling and content are necessary if we are to minister to people where they are.

With some detail, Jesus described how the good Samaritan "bound up his wounds." Point seven: *Effective pastoral care will remedy the hurt.* We can't just express our regrets and go our merry ways. Nor is it good enough for us simply to be with the one who is hurting. You'll notice that the good Samaritan didn't just hold this man's hand and listen to him say how bad he was feeling. Unfortunately, much pastoral care today amounts to little more than that. Whether the hurt is physical or spiritual, there's a need to find a specific strategy which will remedy the situation. This means that on the spiritual level we need to become acquainted with Word-of-God therapies. We need to know how to diagnose and how to treat. We can have all the compassion imaginable, but if we don't know what to do, our compassion isn't worth much. The Bible tells us what to do. For every spiritual struggle, there's an answer—specific and workable. So, if we really care, we need to discover what these answers are.

The next thing we're told is that the good Samaritan "brought him to an inn." Point eight: *Effective pastoral care will bring people to church.* Remember, this man was half dead. That was our condition when we first came to God. We weren't dead *to* sin; we were dead *in* sin. But when we came to church and, more importantly, to Jesus, the Head of the church, all of that changed. God quickened us "who were dead in trespasses and sin" (Eph. 2:1). Which is to say, God made us alive. Now, you and I both know that only God could do this. First Peter 5:8 gives us the alternative, what it's like if we don't receive his care, when it warns: "Your adversary the devil, as a roaring lion, walketh about, seeking whom he may devour." The devil's sole purpose in life is to spiritually kill anyone he can. The wisest thing to do for those people about whom we really care is to bring them to church.

The next step in pastoral care is seen in verse 35. The good Samaritan requested the innkeeper's help. Point nine: *Effective pastoral care will not be a one-man show, but a shared ministry.* God never intended for his pastors to provide all of the pastoral care. But the sad fact is that many pastors do. However, the wise pastor will resist this one-man-show concept of the ministry and will instead devote himself to cultivating a shared ministry.

God has gifted every Christian. If the pastor will equip these already-gifted Christians, his own efforts will be greatly multiplied.

Every pastor has a different set of gifts, and no pastor has all the gifts. This means that the church body needs to minister to those situations when the pastor cannot minister (either because of a limitation on his gifts or because of a limitation on his time). In this instance, the good Samaritan had a limitation on his time; he needed to leave and journey elsewhere.

But notice that the Samaritan said, "I come again" (v. 35). Point ten: *Effective pastoral care involves follow-up.* The good Samaritan didn't just drop the wounded man at the inn and forget him. Instead, after bringing the man to the inn and personally caring for him, the Samaritan found another who could continue the care. Then the Samaritan promised upon his return to follow up and see if this man was well. Unfortunately, much pastoral care—especially as it deals with spiritual problems—fails right here. We simply don't follow up to see if true healing occurs. Follow-up is absolutely important because, in Jeremiah's words: "The heart is . . . desperately wicked: who can know it?" To paraphrase Jeremiah, there's just no telling what the human heart is capable of. It will do whatever it can to resist God's cure. That's why follow-up and accountability are essential. Any minister who ignores this has simply overestimated the human heart.

Did you realize that this story of the good Samaritan had so much in it? The Bible says "care for one another." I think this story helps us to understand—in broad outline anyway—how we're to do that. In summary, our ministry of care will be given to anybody robbed of God's riches, anybody wounded by Satan, and anybody left half-dead in their spirit. We'll minister to these people:

1. by alerting them to the way Satan operates,
2. by enabling them to have a new dignity,
3. by teaching them how to defend themselves against Satan,
4. by remaining alert to our opportunities to minister,
5. by conveying a genuine Christian warmth,
6. by ministering to people where they are,
7. by specifically and practically applying Word-of-God therapies,

8. by bringing them to God's church,
9. by cultivating a shared-ministry effort, and
10. by following up to see if true healing has occurred.

All about us we can hear those in need crying out, in the words of the disciples, "Carest thou not that we perish?" That is the question which really stops us in our tracks. Each of us must allow that question to find its target in our hearts. So, do *you* really care?

5
Comfort One Another

Have you ever watched a movie and become so involved you started to cry or became angry? It's easy to project ourselves into the story, contemplating what we would say or what we would do. Of course, the story was depicted in such a way as to enlist our support.

Nonetheless, in real life, we know that we would be the ones to bring comfort. But we aren't given the luxury of a spectator's role in life. Instead, somebody says or does something and without benefit of the broader view, we react. At the time our reaction seems right. Later, though, it may become clear that we're the culprits in life's drama, causing needless and senseless hurt. That's not what God wants. In fact, in 1 Thessalonians 4:18 he commands, "comfort one another." Let's examine this command, determining the source, the scope, the purpose, and the means of what we call Christian comfort.

The Source of Comfort

Can anybody give comfort? No, I don't think so. Second Corinthians 1:3 refers to our Heavenly Father as "the God of all comfort." This means no one can comfort like God can. The world may try; but what the world has to offer simply doesn't hold up.

For example, have you ever heard somebody say, "Don't worry. Everything will turn out all right." It will? Says who? For the *Christian* "all things work together for good" (Rom. 8:28). But for the world this everything-will-turn-out-all-right philosophy is sheer illusion. In fact, if the people of the world continue to reject God's claim on their lives, they have God's Word for it that everything *won't* turn out all right.

Maybe you've heard somebody say, "Well, give it time. Time will heal." It will? Not by itself. Time is neutral. The fact is many people *don't* improve with time. They become hard, bitter, or plain numb as they drive their anguish into the subconscious realm.

The only comfort the world can give is: "Cheer up—it could be worse." Not much of a comfort, is it? But the world can't promise that troubled times will get better or that problems will eventually work to ultimate good. All the world can do is to observe lamely what everybody knows: It could be worse. What a pallid substitute for Jesus' comfort! "Be of good cheer," he said, "for I have overcome the world." Jesus defeated the powers of darkness. Thus, he and he alone has the resources needed to supply true comfort. When Jesus said, "Be of good cheer," he implied, I think, that there was a cheer that wasn't good. That's the world's cheer. The counterfeit comfort of the world is tantamount to a sugar pill for cancer.

Before ascending to the Father, Jesus said, "I will not leave you comfortless . . . the Father . . . shall give you another Comforter, that he may abide with you forever" (John 14:18,16). Another Comforter? Yes, Jesus ministered a tremendous comfort when he defeated the twin enemies of sin and death. But in his earthly body, Jesus was limited to time and place. The Holy Spirit, however, can minister his comfort anytime, any place. That's why Jesus said, "It is expedient for you that I go away: for if I go not away, the Comforter will not come unto you" (John 16:7). Be clear on this: The only source of true comfort is the Triune God: God the Father, God the Son, and God the Holy Spirit.

The Scope of Comfort

Foundational to God's comfort is his commitment to provide. "The Lord is my Shepherd," David said, "I shall not want." What a comfort to know that all of our needs are going to be met because

Jesus is the Shepherd of our lives. However, David gave us a clearer view into the nature of God's comfort when he continued, "Thy rod and thy staff they comfort me."

What is a rod? What is a staff? The rod was used by shepherds to defend their sheep against an outside attack. Therefore, the rod represents God's capacity to protect. There's no telling where you and I would be today if it weren't for God's protection. You may like the image of being God's sheep because a sheep seems so cuddly, so lovable. But, all due respect, sheep are dumb. So, by likening us to sheep, God has made it plain that in the great warfare over our souls we're hopelessly overmatched. Aren't you thankful, then, for a Shepherd who is willing and able to protect?

To answer the second question, a staff is a thin pole with a crook on the end of it. The staff was used by the shepherd to hook the leg of a straying sheep and put it back on the right course. Therefore, the staff represents God's capacity to direct. Isaiah says, "All we like sheep have gone astray; we have turned every one to his own way" (53:6). That has certainly been true in my own life. So many times God has saved me from myself by redirecting my path.

How good it is to have a God who both protects and directs—a God who meets all of our basic needs (both body and soul), a God who defends us against the two great enemies, the enemy outside (Satan) and the enemy inside (self). Yet, this doesn't mean that God will always make our path easy. He won't. Even the apostle Paul had to report: "We were troubled on every side; without were fightings [that's Satan at work], within were fears [that's self at work]. Nevertheless, God, that comforteth those that are cast down, comforted us" (2 Cor. 7:5-6). Indeed, God's comfort was so supremely adequate that Paul was able to say, "I am filled with comfort . . . in all our tribulation" (2 Cor. 7:4).

What's so good about God's comfort is that it doesn't fade. The Scriptures say that it's "eternal" (2 Thess. 2:16, NIV), that it's forever, and that it leads to a place of complete contentment. "God shall wipe away all tears from their eyes; and there shall be no more death, neither sorrow, nor crying, neither shall there be any more pain: for the former things are passed away" (Rev. 21:4). When will this be? On the last day. And where will it be? In heaven above. What a tender scene: God, like a dear and gentle mother, wiping away our tears. Long ago, God told us he would do this. "As one whom his mother comforteth; so will I comfort you" (Isa. 66:13). Oh, what a day! No more heartache, no more pain. Just like when a mother tells her child, "All well!" Isn't this good? The completeness of God's comfort!

The Purpose of Comfort

The real purpose is to reveal who God is and who we can become.

In the Sermon on the Mount, Jesus said, "Blessed are they that mourn: for they shall be comforted" (Matt. 5:4). What did he mean? By "mourn" Jesus was referring to that state of the soul when in grief over sin. Of course, many people admit to being imperfect, but God wants them to face up to their shortcomings in a more serious way.

Be specific about your sins. Let the truth of who you are sink in. Let it touch your emotions. You're only making a shallow observation when you admit to being imperfect. Many people mourn over the *consequence* of their sin, but not over the *fact* of their sin. Believe me, there is a difference. They yelp to high heaven when their sin finds them out and when they reap what they have sown. But it's not the consequence of your sin that God wants you to mourn over—it's the fact of it. Your sin puts you in league with Satan. It's a slam against the Father. It hurts him. It hurts you. That's what God wants you concerned about.

Let's anticipate the kind of comfort God will give. God will never comfort us by saying, "There, there" to our sins—as if our sins don't matter. Our sins do matter, and God will never overlook them like that. No, when the Bible says we will be comforted, it means our guilt will be taken away. Do you remember the convicting voice of conscience which made you feel rotten inside? Well, by the grace of God, that voice will be hushed. "Though your sins be as scarlet," Isaiah wrote, "they shall be as white as snow" (1:18). In other words, even though our sins are heinous, God can take the guilt away. God can make us pure. God can help us like ourselves. That's part of his comfort. But this comfort will come only when we begin to mourn over our sins and, in our mourning, turn to him.

If you only see yourself, the anguish would remain. But the Holy Spirit's mission is to reveal Jesus: "The Comforter . . . shall testify of me" (John 15:26). "He shall not speak of himself. . . . He shall glorify me" (John 16:13-14). A trademark of biblical comfort is that it always focuses on Jesus—from the very beginning, at the time of our conversion, and all through the rest of our days. Even if we slip, when we're on the verge of giving up, of caving in, God gives us comfort. Paul wrote, "We . . . comforted . . . every one of you . . . that ye would walk worthy of God, who hath called you unto his kingdom and glory" (1 Thess. 2:11). Why does God comfort? To keep us strong, to keep us steady. God's comfort gives us a fresh vision of who we really are.

See the progression? The Comforter works at salvation, during temptation, and through sanctification. *Sanctification* means to be pure, to be put to good use. Let's see how the Holy Spirit intends to use us. Jesus explained the Spirit's ministry:

When he [the Comforter] is come, he will reprove the world of sin, and of righteousness, and of judgment: Of sin, because they believe not on me; of righteousness, because I go to my Father, and ye see me no more; of judgment, because the prince of this world is judged (John 16:8-11).

To interpret this, we must ask, to whom does the Holy Spirit come? To the church? To the world? The answer is that the Spirit comes to the believer! Jesus declared, "The world cannot receive [him], because it seeth him not, neither knoweth him" (John 14:17).

How does the Spirit work in the world? First, he convinces people of sin. Not certain isolated sins, but the great sin of rejecting Jesus! Jesus is the issue. As the Spirit works in the lives of Christians, the world is going to notice.

Second, the Spirit reveals righteousness. Jesus said, "I go to my

Father, and ye see me no more" (John 16:10). With Jesus gone, how is the world going to see righteousness? Simple. There must be a real and noticeable difference in your life and mine. The emphasis here is on an exhibited holiness within the church. Third, the Spirit reveals judgment "because the prince of this world is judged." Again the spotlight is on us. When the world views sin and Satan defeated in our lives, it will begin to suspect that Satan is on the losing side. Seeing that, those outside of Christ will join with Christ.

The purpose of God's comfort, then, is (1) salvation (He takes away guilt and helps us to like ourselves again.), (2) temptation (He catches us when we stumble and puts us back on the right track.), and (3) sanctification (Through us, the world can see what a difference God can make).

The Means

The Bible tells us how, and how not, to give comfort. Let's consider the negative side first. In the book of Job we read about intense suffering. Job lost his health, his wealth, and his family. To the rescue came three friends: Eliphaz, Bildad, and Zophar. We have a detailed account of how they tried to "comfort" Job. But Job called his friends "miserable comforters" (ch. 16). God agreed (ch. 42). To the three would-be comforters God said, "My wrath is kindled against thee . . . for ye have not spoken of me the thing that is right" (42:7). To be frank, they blew it! They tried to comfort, but they only made matters worse. Perhaps, though, we can learn from their mistakes. Let's see what not to do. Point one: *Don't assume.* The three friends assumed the reason for Job's suffering was sin. So they proceeded, almost ruthlessly, to get Job to acknowledge this. But Job would not agree, which only made them madder.

Point two: *Don't just listen to words—be alert to feelings.* Job was under a tremendous strain and by his own admission his words were those of complaint (Job 7:11). Instead of identifying with his feelings, though, his friends seized his words. In a cold, analytical way, they examined everything Job said. We need to be careful because we're sometimes guilty of this. Sometimes, failing to understand another person's hurt, we zero in on the words. This can be devastating. It's important to identify with the anguish which produces the words.

Point three: *Don't say what you don't know.* Job's friends waxed eloquent in their counsel. Much of what they said sounded good. But Job told them they were wrong, and in the end God told them the same thing. C. S. Lewis called what these friends did "Bulverism." According to Lewis, "Bulverism" is attempting to show another person *how* he made his mistake without first establishing if, in fact, he made one. No wonder Job pleaded for silence. Silence would have been far more comforting.

Point four: *Don't overestimate the human heart.* Job's friends underestimated it, but we must also be alert to the equal and opposite mistake. For example, Barnabas. Barnabas was the kind of man you would've liked because he would have liked you. His name meant "son of comfort." And that's what Barnabas was always trying to do. Overlooking the dark side of life (a strange and wonderful approach), Barnabas always tried to be positive. Charming and endearing he was, but it must also be said that a biblical-based comfort must be responsive to the facts, even if the facts are ugly. It's sometimes difficult to receive comfort from someone like Barnabas because, deep down, we know they "look the other way."

To be more positive, let's search the Word to discover how we should give comfort.

In 2 Corinthians 1 we read, "God . . . comforteth us in all our tribulation, that we may be able to comfort them which are in any trouble" (vv. 3-4). Point five: *We must receive God's comfort before we can give it.* Notice Paul said "all" tribulation and "any" trouble. Because Paul had received God's comfort and knew how well it worked, he was able to comfort others. The reason many of us don't know how to give comfort is because we have refused what God has offered. We've tried to muddle through on our own resources. Consequently, when someone else needs help, we're at a loss simply because we ourselves haven't experienced God at this level.

Paul expressed his desire to the Romans to "be comforted to-

gether with you by the mutual faith both of you and me" (1:12).
Point six: *The ministry of Christian comfort must be reciprocal.* The
Scriptures say, "comfort one another." It doesn't say just the
preachers, the deacons, or the Sunday School teachers are to comfort. Everybody, no matter who, is to both give and receive comfort.
The reason not much comfort is given today has to do with our inability to open up and share.

Paul said, "Rejoice with them that do rejoice, and weep with
them that weep" (Rom. 12:15). Point seven: *The one who comforts
must identify with the hurt.* Martin Luther listed affliction as one of
the three essentials of a minister's preparation. He was right. To be
afflicted and to handle the affliction in God's way does prepare one
for ministry. Christian comfort is more than a formula, more than a
philosophy, more even than a Bible verse. Christian comfort is best
received through a person who knows what the hurt is. The Scriptures state that Jesus was "a man of sorrows." So, he knew what it
was to hurt. Paul said, "I know . . . how to be abased" (Phil. 4:12).
So, he knew what it was to hurt. The early Christians were told to
"remember them that are in bonds, as bound with them; and them
which suffer adversity, as being yourselves also in the body" (Heb.
13:3). Elsewhere Paul wrote to consider "thyself lest thou also be
tempted" (Gal. 6:1). The ability to put yourself in the other person's
shoes is immensely important to a ministry of comfort.

Not only that, but Romans 15:4 talks about "the comfort of the
scriptures." Point eight: *Comfort must be given from the Word.* In
the biblical tradition, comfort (which means to call to one's side) is
linked with either consolation (in which you give sympathy) or
exhortation (in which you call for a change of behavior). The important fact is that the Bible *does* have answers and these answers *do*
work. Therefore, the Word *must* be applied to all of our problems.
Interestingly, the Bible links comfort with "being of one mind" (2
Cor. 13:11; Phil. 2:1-2). That's because when we come to have
God's mind on our problems, the result is a deep and lasting comfort.

Point nine: *We need not only the Word but also the Spirit.*

Under the power of the Spirit the Word was written. It's only under the power of the Spirit that the Word is acted upon. In the Greek, the word for "comforter" is the word *Paraclete*. Have you ever gone to one of those counselors who just hears you out, saying "Uh, uh . . . Uh, uh"? There's a widely accepted school of counseling in which the counselor is taught not to give any advice, but to just mirror back what has been said with words like, "I hear you saying . . . " or, "Let me see if this is what you're thinking. . . . " And then your words are given back. Jay Adams is right. "We don't need a parakeet; we need a Paraclete." More than anything else, we need the Spirit to minister his Word. The right perspective and the wrong power leave you right where you are. So don't exclude the Spirit.

No question about it. Life isn't easy. Many people are hurting. So let me ask you: Will you be the one who comforts and consoles? Not lovey, dovey pep talk—but a biblical comfort in the power of the Spirit.

6
Encourage One Another

One of the most neglected ministries of the church is the ministry of encouragement. I'm afraid the old spiritual, "Nobody knows the trouble I've seen, nobody knows but Jesus," describes what's going on.

But let's face it: if nobody knows, it's because we haven't told them. This Lone-Ranger Christianity so popular today is unbiblical. After all, even the Lone Ranger had Tonto! Remember how that spiritual puts it? "Sometimes I'm up, sometimes I'm down." Clearly the Bible tells us what to do during the down times of life. "Encourage each other" (1 Thess. 5:11, TLB). That's the ministry of encouragement.

What is it? Is it finding the sad and mad and telling them jokes? Is it trying to pep people up with our light and festive spirits? Is it getting their minds off their problems through excursion or diversion? That's the way the world goes about it. But the world's encouragement fails in one of three ways. It either (1) underestimates the problem, (2) overestimates the resources, or (3) bypasses the dilemma altogether. But God's encouragement succeeds because it accurately assesses both the person and the problem.

Who Needs Encouragement?

We've trained ourselves to think that we don't need encouragement, but we do. We all have vulnerable moments, moments where we need to be reminded of God's love and the adequacy of his provisions. Interestingly, according to Psalm 64:5, even the wicked need encouraging. "They encourage themselves," David said. Why? Because whether on the side of good or evil, the opposition is still formidable. They encouraged themselves thinking, *who will find us out?* That's a rather contemptible way to live, but it does prove that even the wicked need encouraging.

Who else needs encouragement? Paul exhorted the Thessalonians to "encourage the feebleminded" (1 Thess. 5:14). Now don't get this wrong. By feebleminded, he was not talking about the mentally retarded and the senile. Literally, the word here means the fainthearted, the small-souled—that child of God always being defeated. A person like that can be exasperating, can't he? It's hard. But we're to encourage him reminding him of what God can do. The Bible says he gives endurance to the fainthearted (Isa. 57:15), helping them avoid retreat and defeat.

Do you remember when Joshua became the new leader of the Hebrews? When Joshua was being commissioned, God spoke, Joshua spoke, and then the people spoke. Listen to their words. "According as we hearkened unto Moses in all things, so will we hearken unto thee" (1:17). Sounds good, doesn't it? But if I had been Joshua, I'd have quit right then. Check the record. These people didn't hearken unto Moses. They griped and ventilated their hostility without restraint. However, God knew what it would be like. So twice he gave the command: "Encourage him" (Deut. 1:38; 3:28). Your pastor, your deacons—in fact, all those who minister to you— need encouragement. They do not need vain flattery, just an acknowledgment of how God is working through them.

Why Do We Need Encouragement?

We need encouragement because we all struggle with unbelief. Unbelief doubts the presence of God (Is there a God?), the power of God (Is he able to help me?), the motive of God (Does he want to help me?), or the faithfulness of God (Will he help me?). Most of us don't have any problems with God's presence or power, but we're not as sure about his motive (Does he want to help me?) and even less sure about his faithfulness (Will he help me?). We find an illustration of this in the Old Testament.

And they [meaning the children of Israel] journeyed from mount Hor by way of the Red Sea, to compass the land of Edom: and the soul of the people was much discouraged because of the way. And the people spoke against God, and against Moses, Wherefore have ye brought us up out of Egypt to die in the wilderness? (Num. 21:4-5).

The Israelites were "much discouraged." But why? Because they doubted God's presence? No. His power? No. His motive? Yes! They wanted to know if God brought them into the wilderness to die. Have you ever completely misread a situation? It's easy to do. People used to think the rich had God's favor and the poor didn't. Similarly, they thought the smooth life meant love; the rough, meant wrath. But James said, "Count it all joy when ye fall into divers temptations" (Jas. 1:2). Why? Because when you get into trouble, God can make you "perfect and entire, wanting nothing" (Jas. 1:4). Trouble doesn't mean God is mad at you. The rough, turbulent roads can be character-building.

As Israel neared the Promised Land, Moses said: "The Lord thy God hath set the land before thee: go up and possess it, as the Lord God of thy fathers hath said unto thee; fear not, neither be discouraged" (Deut. 1:21).

"Fear not, neither be discouraged"—a well-worded counsel. Let's see how the people responded: "When they . . . saw the land, they discouraged the heart of the children of Israel, that they should not go into the land" (Num. 32:9).

Does that sound familiar? God told them not to be discouraged. So what did they do? They became discouraged! Their reason? "The people is greater and taller than we; the cities are great and walled up to heaven" (Deut. 1:28).

I wonder if we can find ourselves in this account. Word of the promised land (God's superabundant life) reaches our ears, causing us to get excited. But, upon investigation, we anticipate some big problems! So what do we do? We get scared. We don't even try. We revert back to what's safe, to what's known, never receiving what

God wants to give. Human nature today is exactly what it was in Moses' day. Many come to the edge of what God has promised, admire it, but then turn away thinking, *It just isn't possible. The problems are too great!*

How would you have counseled these discouraged Israelites? As I've studied this, I don't think I can improve on the counsel Moses gave:

Then I said unto you, Dread not, neither be afraid of them. The Lord your God which goeth before you, he shall fight for you, according to all that he did for you in Egypt before your eyes; And in the wilderness, where thou hast seen how that the Lord thy God bare thee, as a man doth bear his son, in all the way that ye went, until ye came into this place. Yet in this thing ye did not believe the Lord your God (Deut. 1:29-32).

Moses first said, "Dread not, neither be afraid." That's because the people were blaming their circumstances. But Moses saw right through that. The real problem wasn't their *circumstance*—it was their *inner stance*. Had their hearts been right, they would have been able to be strong.

Then Moses assured them, "The Lord your God . . . goeth before you" (v. 30). Do you remember what Numbers 21:4 said—they were "much discouraged *because of the way*"? In other words, because of the circumstances. Moses was saying, "Listen, you're not in this alone. God goes with you. And, better still, *before* you, making it possible for you to follow."

The Israelites simply hadn't taken God into account. They looked at the problem and at their resources. Then they turned their backs on it all, thinking the ideal wasn't possible. But Moses said, "Listen, God has already demonstrated that he's bigger than any of your problems. He saved you in Egypt. He has sustained you in the wilderness [v. 31]. So, why are you turning back?" Then Moses answered his own question, "Ye did not believe the Lord your God" (v. 32). Remember, unbelief is always the cause of discouragement.

We know God *can* do great things. We just don't know if he *will*. Can God be counted on to come through *for me?* Can God handle my giant problems? Can God remove the high walls which block me from his promises? Be honest. Isn't it at this level that we have most of our doubting? We doom ourselves to wilderness wandering by not disclosing where we are weak, and not giving those in the body of Christ an opportunity to encourage.

Who needs encouragement? We all do. Why do we need encouragement? Because we all struggle against the sin of unbelief.

What Are We to Do?

Whenever we sense the old Adam coming back and our defenses beginning to fail, a red light ought to flash on: I need encouragement. Pride will urge us to tough it out, but imagine what a tremendous help it would be to have fellow Christians encouraging us with the Word? Jesus said, "Let not your heart be troubled, neither let it be afraid" (John 14:27). You see, the very fact that Jesus is *in* you, and fellow believers *with* you, means you don't have to have a worried and troubled heart. Sure, discouragement may knock, but you can turn it away. Oh, that believers would deepen their friendships and risk the transparency of soul necessary to permit this ministry. It's just this simple—others can't care if we don't share.

The encouragement God wants to give us doesn't just rescue from gloom and doom. It's much more positive. Hebrews 10:24 says, "Consider one another to provoke unto love and to good works." Love relates to the fruit; good works, to the gifts. Love relates to being; good works, to doing. Love relates to fellowship; good works, to ministry. Do you see how comprehensive this is? We're to encourage fellow believers in the development of their inner lives and in the exercising of their gifts. This encouragement, based on the Word and prompted by the Spirit, must be sensitive and sustained. Just a little encouragement works wonders, but a sustained encouragement will transform.

Regrettably, most give encouragement if a loved one goes to the hospital or the morgue. But the encouragement which focuses on the inner man is often missing. Of course this isn't what God wants, but it does raise a question.

What If No One Encourages You?

What if no one encourages you? If that's your predicament, it's not a lost cause because you can follow David's example who, when "greatly distressed . . . encouraged himself in the Lord" (1 Sam. 30:6). This is a tremendous story. David's responsibility had been to guard the city of Ziklag. But the Amalekites invaded the city, burned it to the ground, and took the women and children captive. Needless to say, this defeat produced much weeping and wailing. What made matters worse was that David's own people became so upset that they wanted to stone him. Poor David. He felt utterly wretched and had no one willing to comfort him! Discouragement could have buried him but he didn't allow that to happen. Instead, he relit the candle of hope by encouraging himself in the Lord.

Too many of us allow ourselves to be dragged down with the chariot wheels of circumstance. Bad times come and down we go, the songs of our lives becoming discordant. But it doesn't have to be this way. If no alternative is available, we need to know what to do to encourage ourselves in the Lord.

David didn't moan and groan, asking, "Why did this have to happen?" Many people do that, but David didn't. Nor did he throw dust in the eyes of reason and pretend the problem really didn't bother him. A lot of people attempt to make themselves feel better by denying the problem. But, taking himself in hand, admitting his pain, David lifted his problem to the Lord in prayer. The Bible says, "David inquired at the Lord, saying, Shall I pursue . . . shall I overtake them?" (1 Sam. 30:8). What faith! His home was in ashes, his family was kidnapped, and yet David still believed in God. In effect, David said, "Just give me the word, God. I may not be able to, but you can overcome." God said, "Pursue: for thou shall surely overtake them, and without fail recover all" (1 Sam. 30:8). When God says it's for sure—it's for sure! David did pursue, did overtake, and did recover all (1 Sam. 30:17-18).

In the book of Judges, we read of some others who "encouraged themselves." The children of Israel had just suffered a bitter defeat at the hands of Benjamin. Twenty-two thousand men had died. But like David, these people asked counsel of the Lord, saying, "Shall I go up again to battle against the children of Benjamin?" Such wisdom! They neither resigned themselves to defeat nor presumed to know what to do. So they asked for God's counsel. And the Lord said, "Go up against him" (20:23). Once more they sought victory, but they lost! Eighteen thousand men died! At this point, most of us would have given up. But they knew God was in control so they sought his counsel once more.

Interestingly, God did not rebuke them for their defeat. God did not predict victory the first time. He wanted them in the struggle, but he knew there would be no victory yet. Doesn't that speak volumes? We each may be in a struggle right now due to no fault of our own. We may have experienced some painful setbacks—again, due to no fault of our own. But let's not give up. God is still in control and he means for us to win.

Israel asked what you and I would have asked, "Shall I cease?" In other words, shall I give up? But the Lord said *no!* "For tomorrow I will deliver" (Judg. 20:28). And as we read on (Judg. 20:20-48), that's exactly what happened. "Tomorrow I will deliver" . . . not today, but *tomorrow*. Could that be God's counsel to you? I know this struggle is hard. I know it seems as if tomorrow will never come. But encourage yourself. In the words of Jesus, "Men ought always to pray, and not to faint" (Luke 18:1). The victory may not come today. But it will come!

A second way that encouragement comes is through the Word. *The New International Version* says that we "can encourage . . . by sound doctrine" (Titus 1:9). Second Timothy 4:2 says that "in season, and out of season" we are to "encourage" with "careful instruction" (NIV). The opposite of fainting (that is of discouragement) is "to gird up the loins." First Peter 1:13 says, "Gird up the loins of your mind." Ephesians 6:14 says, "having your loins girt about with truth." Girding up the loins symbolizes a readiness to fight. When the Roman soldier prepared for battle, the first thing he did was to tuck the tunic under his belt so his legs could be unimpeded for battle. Notice: Peter talks about the loins of *the mind.* And Ephesians says we are to gird up the loins *with truth.* So if you want to stand your ground and win the victory, you must prepare by digging into the Word. Let the Word do what it says it will do: encourage you!

But what is the basis of this encouragement? It has to do with your position in Christ. David encouraged himself "in the Lord." Not "by" the Lord or "with" the Lord or "through" the Lord, but "in" the Lord. Corresponding to that is Paul's favorite New Testament term, "*in* Christ." Once you become a Christian, once you're in Christ, it's a brand-new ball game. In his book *I'm OK; You're OK,* Thomas Harris says 96 percent of the population has "not OK" feelings about themselves. According to Harris, most people struggle with feelings of inferiority; most are easily discouraged. But for the Christian—if he'll only believe and receive—it doesn't have to be that way. Philippians 2:1 talks about the consolation ("encouragement," NIV) of being "in Christ." What is this consolation? What is its basis?

Romans 3:24 talks about "being justified freely . . . through the redemption that is in Christ Jesus." Romans 8:1 says, "There is therefore now no condemnation to them which are in Christ Jesus." This means that because of our position in Christ, God holds nothing against us. Whenever we begin to feel that God is mad at us or that God doesn't care, we can chase away that feeling with the truth. Ephesians 1:6 says that we're "accepted in the Beloved." Now, if our acceptance before God were based on our performance, we would have cause to be uneasy. But it's not. Our acceptance is based on Christ's performance. Because of that, we may, once and for all, know that God cares.

Romans 8:2 says that "the law of the Spirit of life in Christ Jesus hath made me free from the law of sin and death." This verse teaches that because of our position in Christ not only are we free from the wages of sin (death) but also free from sin itself. This doesn't mean that we'll be sinless, but it does mean that the Spirit is stronger than sin and that no sin needs to defeat us. Isn't that encouraging?

Colossians 1:2 states, "Brethren in Christ . . . grace be unto you, and peace." We often think nothing that good will ever happen; but according to this verse, we can expect the unexpected—grace. And if trouble does come, we can discover an inner serenity of soul even in the midst of conflict. And why all of this? Because we're "in Christ!"

Second Corinthians 2:14 declares, "Thanks be unto God, which always causeth us to triumph in Christ." That's a powerful statement. The world says, You win some; you lose some. Wrong! If you are in Christ; you can win them all!

Ephesians 1:3 teaches that "God . . . hath blessed us with all spiritual blessings . . . in Christ." If we're Christian, every blessing can be ours . . . every single one! But frequently we say, "I haven't received them." That's because believing means receiving and we're not believing. What we need to do is make our claims in his name.

Philemon 8 promises that we can be "bold in Christ." First Timothy 3:13 speaks of "great boldness . . . in Christ." So what does this say about our inferiority complexes? It says that if we'll reckon who we really are in Christ (not who we are in our own right) we can face life with an entirely new perspective. Be clear on this. Boldness isn't the flashy, dedicated zeal of the flesh. Boldness isn't being the ones out front, getting people to do what we want by our extraordinary capacities and charm. The fact is, we can be shy, quiet, and reticent, but bold. Boldness is the ability to see God's dream and the availability to be used of God to the extent that the dream comes true. It's easy to become "weary in well doing" (Gal. 6:9). We do our best, hanging in there long after others have quit. But we get discouraged. Yet, if we're in Christ we can say with the apostle Paul, "Through God's mercy we have this ministry, we do not lose heart" (2 Cor. 4:1, NIV). "We faint not; [for] . . . the inward man is renewed day by day" (2 Cor. 4:16). Renewed in what way? We are renewed with God's presence, perspective, and power! Boldness—it can come only from God's power.

Jude 1:1 says that we are "preserved in Jesus Christ." Ephesians 1:12-13 says that those "in Christ . . . were sealed with that holy Spirit of promise." Romans 8:39 tells us that nothing will "be able to separate us from the love of God, which is in Christ Jesus our Lord." I encourage you to read everything in the Bible about you who are in Christ. There are more than seventy tremendous verses which describe a reality that we need to tap. If you want, you can stay in your ho-hum ways—and no doubt, just as you had hoped, you'll make it to heaven. Why? Because God has preserved and sealed you. But heaven can come into you, and you can live in the glow of a continual encouragement if you'll only believe what God has declared to be true about who you are in Christ.

If you ever receive the ministry of encouragement, you'll wonder how you ever lived without it. God wouldn't have said this much about encouragement if you and I didn't need it. Wouldn't it be marvelous if this ministry were cultivated in our churches? It was said of Judas and Silas that they "said much to encourage and strengthen the brothers" (Acts 15:32, NIV). What a powerful ministry . . . this ministry of encouragement! And you can have a part in it if you are "in Christ."

7
Greet One Another

It's been said that we evangelicals are the "greetingest, eating-est, meetingest," folk anywhere on God's good earth. If we're going to do that, let's do it right. Let's find out not what the Bible says about eating or meeting—though it has a good deal to say about both—but what the Bible teaches about greeting. God actually commanded us to greet one another.

What can be so strategic about giving a greeting? Words of welcome are nice, but nice enough to warrant five commands? Yes, I think so. God didn't mean the kind of greeting that is merely a pleasant exchange of polite words, acknowledging another's presence. "Good morning!" you say, almost upon instinct.

"Good morning!" your friend repeats in a hurried, mechanical manner. "How are you?"

"Oh, just fine," you assure him, "just fine." And before you're aware of it, you've continued on your way and your friend has continued on his. Very courteously, each has greeted the other. But surely this isn't the greeting which God is anxious for us to share.

Such niceties may contribute to warmth and friendliness, but there's nothing particularly Christian about them. Maybe your friend wasn't really wanting to know how you were doing. And perhaps you weren't about to tell him. I don't mean to demean the cordial language of public life, but can't it be rather superficial? Does this mean, then, that we need to be more enthusiastic in our greetings, giving a great big "Howdee!" like Minnie Pearl? Enthusiasm wouldn't hurt, and I'm sure that Minnie is not only warm and funny but also sincere. But that's not what makes a greeting "Christian."

What does make a greeting "Christian"? If enthusiasm and sincerity aren't the critical factors, what are? Must we employ the language of Zion in our greetings—some Hallelujah-praise-the-Lord!-God-bless-you-brother talk? No, that's not the critical factor either. But while we're on the subject of the language of Zion, let me speak a word of caution. Restraint may be necessary in this area because not only is our evangelical talk a "turn off" to some people but it may also be a "turn off" to God. That could be especially true if our language becomes flippant "code" words which identify us as a part of some inner group. I've heard some good Christians say, "Glory!" and "Praise Jesus" when their favorite athletic team won. This is not what Jesus wants.

Returning to our question, What makes a greeting Christian? A greeting becomes Christian when it acknowledges another person—not just for being there, not just for being likeable, not just for being accomplished—for who he or she is in Jesus Christ. Quite clearly, the Bible talks about two kinds of greetings—one which is Christian and one which is not. Let's examine these two kinds of greetings.

The World's Greeting

The world greets people for at least one of three reasons: (1) because they are present, (2) because they are popular, or (3) because they are preeminent. Most will greet another person simply because he is present. However, some people, perhaps wanting to climb the social ladder, will go out of their way to greet the person who is popular. Of course, others will make a special attempt to greet the person who has excelled in one endeavor or another. Unfortunately, the religious leaders of Jesus' day fell into this third category. They wanted people to greet them with a flattery which recognized their moral excellence.

Jesus said of the scribes and the Pharisees:

But all their works they do for to be seen of men: they make broad their phylacteries, and enlarge the borders of their garments, and

love the uppermost rooms at feasts, and the chief seats in the synagogues, and greetings in the markets, and to be called of men,
Rabbi, Rabbi (Matt. 23:5-7).

How easily we can fall into this trap. We come into God's church
wanting only to give praise and honor to his name. But somewhere
along the way, people begin to notice the improvement God is making; they see now he has gifted us. And then before you know it, it's
not God's name we're thinking about—it's our own! We become
addicted to the praises others heap on our names. Indeed, being
noticed becomes such a ruling passion that we do what we do so
others will notice us. And if for some reason they don't notice us sufficiently, we pout, sulk, and grow sullen and sour.

Some ministers will violate the most sacred commands if it will
promote their esteem in the eyes of the denomination. One pastor
lamented, "I sold my soul in order to become vice-president of the
convention." Of course, this isn't simply a pastor's problem. We're all
guilty of doing the Lord's work for inferior motives. So often it's *our*
name that we want praised, not the Lord's.

Our Lord had some very stern words about the religious person
who acts like that: "Beware of the scribes, which desire to walk in
long robes, and love greetings in the markets, and the highest seats
in the synagogues, and the chief rooms at feasts" (Luke 20:46).
Jesus also said: "Woe unto you, Pharisees! for ye love the uppermost seats in the synagogues, and greetings in the markets" (Luke
11:43).

Notice that recurring phrase—"greetings in the markets." These
religious leaders loved that extra courtesy they received when those
in the marketplace spoke their names. "Good morning, Rabbi. It's so
good to see you today." Ah, the reverence of tone and the twinkle of
eye which accompanied those words caused the good rabbi to strut
with expanded chest and elevated chin. But the greeting the rabbi
wanted was not one which had its focus on God and the good work
he was doing.

No, the rabbi was wanting a greeting which focused on him.

"Tell me I'm wonderful" was the title of his life script. "I know words will fail you, but try." What made matters worse was that those religious leaders were living out this life script in God's name. *Have we followed in their steps? Do we do the Lord's work with a ready ear for compliments?* Of course, there's nothing wrong with a genuine compliment, unless we want them too much, like the scribes and the Pharisees did. Though it's sobering, I think we have a clear word from the Lord about what will happen to any of us if we become puffed up with our own bloated sense of self-esteem. In Acts 12 we read:

And upon a set day Herod, arrayed in royal apparel, sat upon his throne, and made an oration unto them. And the people gave a shout, saying, It is the voice of a god, and not of a man. And immediately the angel of the Lord smote him, because he gave not God the glory: and he was eaten of worms, and gave up the ghost (vv. 21-23).

Now, that's a rather drastic response! Herod accepted some undue compliments and for that God took him! You say, "God did that to wicked old Herod, but what's that got to do with us?" Plenty! Notice six things about Herod: (1) He was arrayed in royal apparel. The Scriptures say that the scribes drew attention to themselves by walking "in long robes." (2) He sat upon his throne. The Scriptures say that the Pharisees loved "the chief seats," "the highest seats." (3) He made an oration. The Scriptures indicate that both scribes and Pharisees "for a pretense" gave long public prayers. (4) He allowed people to think he was a god. The Scriptures say that the Pharisees also tried to impress the people with their godlikeness. For we're taught that they "made broad their phylacteries." In other words, in large letters, they printed Scripture on the parchments which they wore in an attempt to convince people of how holy they were. The borders of a garment were a reminder to the Jews that they were a peculiar people (Num. 15:38). But that wasn't good enough for the Pharisees. They wanted everybody to know just how unique and special they really were. They "enlarged the borders of their garments." (5) Herod "gave not God the glory." Were the Pharisees any different? Weren't they trying to win earthly praise in every conceivable fashion? And (6) we're told that Herod was "eaten of worms." Jesus said that the scribes and the Pharisees would "receive the greater condemnation" (Matt. 23:14; Luke 20:47). He didn't spell it out, but that condemnation must be pretty bad.

Clearly then we're left with the unalterable conviction that Jesus was intensely negative about the greetings of the world. For these greetings are either inadequate (in that they acknowledge little more than one's presence) or sinful (in that they give praise to man and not God).

The Greetings of the Church

However, how does a "Christian" greeting differ from the greeting of the world? It differs in two ways: first, in terms of its depth and second, in terms of its context. Let's first examine the difference in depth.

You are well aware that we communicate with one another on various levels. The surface level is the level on which most of our greetings are exchanged. Our hellos and good-byes are almost always a ritual in that we often give them with no real thought. Usually when we consider greeting people, we think about it on this level. So, in our minds "greet one another" means "be warm, sociable, and friendly; be a good mixer." While there's something to say about this capacity to engage others, this is not what the Bible is talking about when it says "greet one another."

Another level of communication is what we might call pastimes. Pastimes are superficial exchanges between people (very often used at parties). This level is somewhat deeper than the level of ritual, but it still bypasses a meaningful, interpersonal exchange. The fact is that many people don't want to relate to others at a deeper level. If they can merely have "topic security" (that is, if they can just talk about a subject with which they are familiar), that's all they want.

Still another level of communication is what we call intimacy. Intimacy involves a sharing that goes deeper than the ritual or pastime levels. Intimacy involves a sharing of your own inner life. But because intimacy involves vulnerability, and maybe even rejection, many people prefer the other levels of communication (the ritual or the pastime) or, worse still, no communication (an activity or a withdrawal). I'm convinced that it's the intimate level of communication which is foundational to the scriptural command: "Greet one another." The hello-nice-to-see-you-come-back level of greeting is OK. But that's not what these five biblical commands had in mind. The Christian greeting isn't just a nicety. It is based on a sharing, bearing relationship.

The longest greeting list in the Scriptures is found in Romans 16. If you'll read through that list, you'll see by Paul's many terms of endearment that this is not "small talk" on the ritual level, for there is a shared intimacy behind each greeting. For example, Paul called Phebe "our sister" (v. 1). He called Priscilla and Aquila "my helpers" (v. 3). He spoke of "my well-beloved Epaenetus" (v. 5). Andronicus and Junia were called "my fellow prisoners" (v. 7). Paul spoke of Amplias, "my beloved in the Lord" (v. 8). He spoke of Stachys as "my beloved" (v. 9). He referred to the "beloved Persis" (v. 12) and said that the mother of Rufus has been like a mother to him (v. 13).

There's absolutely no telling how many intimate experiences lie behind these simple greetings. This was not the surface greeting of some distant acquaintances. No, Paul enjoyed a beautiful relationship with each one. Other passages stress the same truth (Col. 4:10; Philem. 20-23). These heartfelt greetings spring from intimacy, not from the rehearsed politeness of ritual.

The second way the greeting of the church differs from the greeting of the world is in terms of context. The world's greetings pay homage to the winsomeness of personality or the impressiveness of achievement. But the church's greeting, while appreciating both personality and achievement, couches its appreciation in a God-at-work theology. For example, (returning to Romans 16), Paul called Phebe "a servant of the church . . . [who] has been a great help to many people" (vv. 1-2, NIV). Then he wrote of Priscilla and Aquila,

"They risked their lives for me" (vv. 3-4, NIV). He said, "Greet Mary who bestowed much labour on us" (v. 6). "Salute Urbane, our helper in Christ" (v. 9). "Salute Apelles approved in Christ" (v. 10) and then, "Salute Tryphena and Tryphosa, who labour in the Lord" (v. 12). Of course, many other verses could be cited which show Paul greeting those who have achieved in the Lord's work.

How does the praise linked to Paul's greetings differ from the praise given to the Pharisees? There were many differences between the Pharisees and the early Christians which help to explain this. First, the Pharisees weren't really doing the Lord's work. Second, what they did, they did for the wrong reason. Jesus said all their works were done "to be seen of men." And, third, what they did, they did in the wrong power, their own! Scan the first thirteen verses of Romans 16. The term "in Christ" or its equivalent "in the Lord" is used nine times. This term carries with it the theology that God is at work determining plans, determining goals, and determining results. The greeting Paul gave does recognize significant achievement, but always in the context of God at work. In this way, then, Paul's greeting did not lead to pride, but the greeting that the Pharisees wanted did.

So, how does the church's greeting differ from the world's? In two ways. They differ in depth. The world's greeting is more ritual; the church's greeting is more intimate. And they differ in context. The world's greeting praises a man in his own right; the church's greeting praises a man for who he is in the Lord. This difference in depth and context is so decisive that John warned not to give a Christian greeting to a person who is not in Christ.

If there come any unto you, and bring not this doctrine [that Jesus Christ came in the flesh], receive him not into your house, neither bid him God speed: For he that biddeth him God speed is partaker of his evil deeds (2 John 10-11).

These aren't the words of some narrow-minded bigot. The apostle of love spoke these words because the Christian greeting is intended for Christians, not for the world.

The Holy Kiss

The verse from which this chapter title came reads in full, "All the brethren greet you. Greet ye one another with an holy kiss" (1 Cor. 16:20; 2 Cor. 13:12; Rom. 16:16). First Thessalonians 5:26 says: "Greet all the brethren with an holy kiss." First Peter 5:14 expands the command, saying, "Greet ye one another with a kiss of charity."

One of the pleasures of serving in Hawaii was that we always greeted our visitors with a kiss. I don't know how holy it was, but it surely was nice! Seriously, though, are we under command to employ the holy kiss? No, I don't think so. There's a difference between form and function. Form changes from generation to generation or from culture to culture. But function doesn't change. In this instance, the form of a holy kiss was and is very acceptable in the Middle East. But it's not our custom in this land, so the form is not binding. However, the function is. Greeting fellow Christians with a genuine warmth and affection is desirable; indeed, it's commanded for *every* Christian and *every* church. This is the heart of the matter.

In most churches, most Christians don't feel a genuine warmth and affection for each other. They may not be hostile to one another, but, with rare exception, whenever the name of a certain church member comes up, their first thought may be critical. This is particularly true of churches with a stable membership.

These people, having lived together for years, have had so many experiences with each other that, very predictably, at one time or another each has rubbed the other the wrong way. Very often it was only a minor matter, a misunderstanding that could have been cleared up immediately if only those involved had taken the trouble to do so. But instead church members have stockpiled these little grievances. With unfortunate accuracy they've memorized the whole inventory! Mention a certain person's name, and memory will replay the entire episode. Feelings of hurt and anger will stew and brew and, though none of this may come out, there's a definite emotional blockage toward that other person.

I'm not talking about grave injustices. I'm referring to little things—something said that you didn't feel was right, something someone did which you disagreed with. But you remember them. True, if you were to explain what it is that bothers you about this person, you could say a lot of good things too. We usually do say good things if only to keep people from thinking that we're too petty. Nonetheless, the fact remains that there's a certain emotional blockage between us and other people. I suspect that, at best, only a few people don't struggle with this problem. We may be polite and cordial, but minor problems restrain us from greeting some people with the emotional release of contagious joy.

What keeps this problem entrenched in us is the nearly universal denial of the problem. I don't know how many times church members have shared with me some minor grievances relating to other church members, only to reject the scriptural counsel of working it out with the persons involved by saying, "No, I'm not that upset. It will work itself out." Then, why hasn't it?

These minor problems don't work themselves out because perhaps we're too sensitive in the first place. A fragile ego is easily bruised. Second, when we're hurt, we don't do anything about it. Part of our thinking says the problem is too petty, so the best thing to do is to just forget about it. But another part of us won't let us forget the problem. That means one of two things: Either the problem isn't petty and, therefore, must be dealt with in a scriptural manner, or we really are too sensitive and must acknowledge that oversensitivity is really the problem.

If the relationship must be dealt with through loving confrontation, then deal with it that way. Don't sweep it under the rug and pretend it didn't happen. It *did* happen and it *has* affected you. The refusal to forgive is bad enough. But not to give a fellow believer a chance for forgiveness is even worse! It means we don't care enough about the relationship even to try to work it out.

The Bible says, "The little foxes, . . . spoil the vines" (Song of Sol. 2:15). In other words, little problems can ruin a church. If you want to understand just how devastating these little problems can be to a church, ask yourself, *How many people in my church am I really wanting to get to know in a deep, intimate way?* Take some time to reflect on this question before answering it. Then ask yourself, *How many people in this church do I not want to know in a deep, intimate way?* (See "Doing the Word," chapter 7, for more instructions on using these questions as a personal exercise.) You were probably able to think of more people you would rather not be close to than people you would like to get to know better. If this is true, something is holding you back. God wants to help you improve these relationships. After all, he commanded us to "greet one another."

The Christian greeting is offered in the context of intimacy. The Christian greeting is offered in the context of a God-at-work theology. The Christian greeting is offered in the context of joy. The Christian greeting is offered to every Christian. The Bible says "one another" and "all the brethren." Will you meet this challenge? Will you do your part to make each relationship right in the Lord? God wants us to be the greetingest, meetingest, and eatingest folk on earth. But the meeting and the eating will mean nothing unless we resolve to do things God's way and, in his love, "greet one another."

8
Honor One Another

One of the basic needs of the humans is the need for respect. Life becomes rancid and sour if this need isn't met. The Bible, more than any other book, tells us how to meet it. Hebrews 2:7 says: "Thou [meaning God] madest him [meaning man] a little lower than the angels; thou crownedst him with glory and honour." When we came from the hand of God, we represented the pinnacle of creation. In fact, what Hebrews 2:7 says about us, Hebrews 2:9 says about Jesus, "a little lower than the angels . . . crowned with glory and honour." What a comparison! God wanted us to be like Jesus. Honor and glory are due us! Or, as one person put it, "I know I'm somebody because God don't make no junk!" It may not be good grammar, but it's a great truth.

God means for each of us to be somebody special because in God's eyes we are special! Don't settle for a deflated self-image. Don't fritter life away in thankless neglect. Don't tear down what God wants to build up. We each need to expand our horizons according to God's image of us!

Why are we each special? Is it because of personality? ability? or willingness to please? The world uses the criteria of performance, but the Scriptures say we're special because of what God has done. "Thou [God] crownedst him [us] with glory and honor." The reason we're special is because of God.

If we were special for any reason other than God, our sense of worthwhileness would yo-yo up and down. What a sad sight to watch athletes living in the shadow of fame, many vainly trying for a comeback. Once they were in the spotlight, but now they're among the discarded heroes of the past. When honor and glory are based upon performance, they become rare and fleeting commodities. When our glory and honor are based on God, they become stabilizing reassurance because "God is the same yesterday, today, and for ever."

The Wrong Kind of Honor

Jesus was very specific about where his honor came from. He said, "I receive not honour from men" (John 5:41). The opinion of others didn't matter to Jesus because the crowd isn't always right. Some called Jesus a devil (Mark 3:22); some, a great prophet (Matt. 16:14); some, the Lord God of the universe (John 1:1-4). How's that for a mixed review! If Jesus had based his worthwhileness on what others thought of him, he'd have been on an emotional roller coaster, never sure where he stood. That's what happens to people who take their sense of worth strictly from the assessment of others.

Jesus said, "How can ye believe, which receive honour one of another, and seek not the honour that cometh from God only?" (John 5:44). Jesus was teaching that there's conflict between what the world thinks and what God thinks. That being so, Jesus wondered out loud how people could call themselves disciples if they were more concerned about the approval of others than of God.

This raises the question: to whom do we play our lives? When we get up in the morning, commencing our activities for the day, whom do we want to please—loved ones? friends? people who can advance our cause? or God? If our focus scarcely goes beyond the visible and the immediate, we won't be thinking about God's will. Instead, our agenda will come totally from the natural. The acid test of belief is to listen to the beat of a different drummer, to become prayerfully alert to God's will, to make every decision in light of his Word. We should live to please God, not the crowd.

In Numbers 24:11, the wicked king, Balak, told the wicked prophet, Balaam, "I thought to promote thee unto great honour;

but, lo, the Lord hath kept thee back from honour." Clearly, then, there's an honor the Lord doesn't want us to have; and sometimes he'll intervene, just as he did with Balaam, in order to keep us from it. The only honor worth having is "the honour that cometh from God only" (John 5:44).

Some say, "It's not what other people think, it's what you think." No, Jesus said, "If I honour myself, my honour is nothing" (John 8:54). Jesus Christ, the perfect Son of God, a constant delight to his Father, supremely adequate in every way, said that he couldn't establish his own worth; it wouldn't mean anything. The only opinion that counts is God's. "It is my Father that honoureth," Jesus said. Honor and glory come from God!

There are three kinds of honor: honor from man, honor from self, and honor from God. By the sheer force of language in John 8:54 and 5:44 (notice the words "nothing" and "only"), we're forced to conclude that there isn't much compatibility among the three. We need to examine ourselves, our motives, to discover whom we live for. Most of us never do that until pain exposes the shallows where we've been adrift.

Honor Among Believers

You've heard it said: "There's honor among thieves." Perhaps not as much as there used to be now that plea bargaining is here, but even the criminal world has some semblance of honor. God wants his church to be a fellowship where believers "honor one another" (Rom. 12:10, NIV). The King James translation reads, "in honor preferring one another." What does this mean? It means that instead of being preoccupied with our agenda—our needs, our wants, our plans, our goals— we'll give preference to our fellow believer: his needs, his wants, his plans, his goals. Little of this is seen in our churches today. Our busy, overcrowded lives have stalemated a lot of relationships. But, according to Romans 12:10, we must respond by actively seeking to bless. The phrase "preferring one another" literally means "to go before another." That is taking the initiative to meet his needs, not waiting on him to meet ours. Our prayer should be, "Lord, show me how I can bless, how I can meet another Christian's needs."

We perk up and take notice when the Bible teaches us how special we are. But when it comes to honoring someone else, especially someone we don't like, the temptation is to filter it out, to file it away, and in planned neglect to refuse to act. Listen, we'll never experience the exhilaration of good overcoming evil unless we venture out of our ego-protecting turtle shells and do what the natural will never do—give honor to believers who rub us raw. How? By recognizing what is good, by looking for ways to bring the goodness out, by expressing appreciation whenever it appears.

Have you ever listened to Rodney Dangerfield? This rubbery-faced comedian with sad, hound-dog eyes is famous for the line "I don't get no respect." That touches something deep in the human spirit. When we were young, our parents praised us for the least little thing, but now no one says very much. Something's wrong with our adult world that is all too ready to find fault and very slow to give praise. Even the church is distressingly blind to incredible goodness.

Jesus said, "A prophet is not without honour, save in his own country, and in his own house" (Matt. 13:57). We overlook much good. Many, I suspect, will be utterly surprised when, on that last day, God gives glorious honor to people grossly underrated down here. People in your church and mine are going to be exalted in that day. Because of our penchant for finding fault, because of our inability to appreciate good, we just aren't enjoying these people like God is.

How to Honor

"Let nothing be done through strife or vainglory" (Phil. 2:3). The Scriptures are clear, "Agree with one another so that there may be no divisions among you" (1 Cor. 1:10, NIV). No fighting in the church! When brothers and sisters get along, it's a tribute to the parents. It is the same in the church. When we love other believers, the glory goes to God. Notice the links between strife and vainglory? Usually when we have a fuss, vainglory is what prompted it or, at the very least, sustained it. That is, somebody is protecting his pride, somebody is defending her territory, somebody wants to win. The Bible suggests a better way.

"But in lowliness of mind let each esteem other[s] better than themselves" (Phil. 2:3). Esteem is what we all want, so let's be Christian enough to give it instead of fighting for it. This verse takes us one step beyond the Golden Rule. The Golden Rule says: "As ye would that men should do to you, do ye also to them likewise" (Luke 6:31). But this verse says, do *more* for others than you do for you. To follow this teaching would eliminate all ugliness in the church.

"Look not every man on his own things but every man also on the things of others" (Phil. 2:4). This calls for a change of focus, a focus we can't have unless there's an actual change within. "Let this mind be in you, which was also in Christ Jesus" (v. 5). The natural mind balks at the command to do more for others than for self. The solution is to let God change our minds! "Let this mind," the mind of Jesus Christ, "be in you"! Now, let's see how this mind works. "Who, being in the form of God, thought it not robbery to be equal with God: But made himself of no reputation, and took upon him the form of a servant, and was made in the likeness of men" (vv. 6-7). Jesus could have stayed in heaven, letting sinful humanity get what it deserved. But he didn't do that. Instead, with no pride, he became of no reputation. And, even though he didn't have to, he identified with us in the closest of ways, suffering what he never deserved —"the death of the cross."

"Oh," but you say, "if I esteemed others better than myself that would be dangerous, I'd lose out." No, you wouldn't. For after Jesus suffered a shameful death, "God also hath highly exalted him" (v. 9). If we'll just quit worrying about our concerns and give of ourselves to others, God will exalt us. Until we see as Jesus saw, we won't do as he did. Giving honor, I submit, is directly proportionate to the degree that Christ's mind is in us.

How to Be Honored

We've talked about the honor God wants us to have and the honor he wants us to give, now let's come at this from a different angle. How do we gain God's honor? A most instructive passage is Mark 10. The end was near. Jesus was on his way to Jerusalem. But James and John weren't thinking about that. Instead, they came to Jesus asking, "Master, we would that thou shouldest do for us whatsoever we shall desire." Kind of a blank check. Sign it, Lord. We'll fill in the amount.

But Jesus wasn't put off by that because he wants us to set our sights high. In his own words, "With God all things are possible" (Mark 10:27). "And he said unto them, What would ye that I should do for you? They said unto him, Grant unto us that we may sit, one on thy right hand, and the other on thy left hand, in thy glory" (Mark 10:36-37).

So what were they wanting? Power, prestige, preeminence. In a word, honor! To us it all sounds so selfish. But, notice, nowhere in this passage does Jesus rebuke them. That's because God's highest honor *is* a worthy goal. So, in response, Jesus simply redirected their thinking on how to obtain such honor.

But Jesus said unto them, Ye know not what ye ask: can ye drink of the cup that I drink of? and be baptized with the baptism that I am baptized with? And they said unto him, We can. And Jesus said unto them, Ye shall indeed drink of the cup that I drink of; and with the baptism that I am baptized withal shall ye be baptized: But to sit on my right hand and on my left hand is not mine to give; but it shall be given to them for whom it is prepared (Mark 10:38-40).

The cup? The baptism? What was Jesus talking about? The psalmist sang, "my cup runneth over." To him, then, the cup was something positive, something which takes place within the realm of our experience. But Jesus prayed, "Father, . . . remove this cup." To him, the cup was something negative, something so bitter, so galling that no one would ever want it. Baptism, of course, means to be immersed, that which touches every area of life. Like the cup, it also conjures up images of suffering. The Old Testament speaks of passing through deep waters.

The equation Jesus presented here is the cup and baptism on one side—God's reserved seat of honor on the other. In other words, the closer we get to Christ the crucified the closer we'll get to Christ the glorified. If that's true, no wonder Paul prayed, "That I might know him . . . and the fellowship of his suffering." But Jesus makes it clear. This isn't marching orders for masochism. The suffering, as well as the honor, is determined by God.

We claim we want honor; but do we really know what we're asking for? In Jesus's words, "Can ye drink of the cup . . . and be baptized with the baptism?" All too often focusing on the crown—not the cross—we answer with the brothers, "We can." "Sure, Lord, whatever. Bring it on. We'll handle it." Sort of sounds like a little boy, bragging about how he can win the war. But Jesus didn't douse the dream. Instead, with real tenderness, he looked down the corridors of the future, seeing how the Spirit would strengthen, seeing how the two would be martyred: James beheaded by the sword and John boiled in oil. I wonder if in much the same way God sees his Spirit doing a tremendous work through you. For now, you may be so naive, so faithless. But God has plans for you. So, before its over, your life's going to be a powerful witness.

Don't misread what Jesus was saying. Honor isn't just a matter of how you die. It's a matter of life-style. In the words which follow, our Lord made this clear.

Ye know that they which are accounted to rule over the Gentiles exercise lordship over them; and their great ones exercise authority upon them. But so shall it not be among you: but whosoever will be great among you, shall be your minister: And whosoever of you will be chiefest, shall be servant of all. For even the Son of man came not to be ministered unto, but to minister, and to give his life a ransom for many (Mark 10:42-45).

The world sees honor as belonging to titled persons, those able to command, to those compelling others to act. Jesus rejected the pomposity of that honor. His honor comes through service. You see, when we minister to someone else, that ministry, and the love which motivated it, gives us a place of honor in that other person's life. Not the honor announced by trumpets, but something far deeper and much more satisfying.

The story which follows seems to represent an abrupt change of subject. Most commentators see no connection. To them, Mark simply chronicles what happened next. But we know we're not merely dealing with chronology because this is where the story of Zacchaeus fits in, but Mark omits it. Instead, inspired by God, Mark told this story.

And they came to Jericho: and as he went out of Jericho with his disciples and a great number of people, blind Bartimaeus, the son of Timaeus, sat by the highway side begging. And when he heard that it was Jesus of Nazareth, he began to cry out, and say, Jesus, thou son of David, have mercy on me (Mark 10:46-47).

What does this account with Bartimaeus have to do with what James and John were asking? God gives us a clue. Notice the double designation: "Bartimaeus, the son of Timaeus." *Bar* simply means "son of." So by giving the name twice God was saying, "There's something here I want you to see." *Timaeus* means honor. And what were James and John asking for? Honor! And did they know what that was? No, like Bartimaeus, they were "blind." Continue reading the passage and you'll see the two stories structurally related in that Jesus asked Bartimaeus the same question he put to the brothers, "What wilt thou that I should do unto thee?"

Perhaps you can see yourself in this story. Maybe you feel like a nobody on the road of life, the easily unnoticed one, unblessed by the advantages of others, on the sidelines, nothing really happening. But through his Word, the Lord God of the universe confronts you with this astounding question, "What do you want me to do for you?" Those words ought to drive to your inner depths. What *do* you want God to do? Do you want the world's honor—the fanfare of royalty, the popularity of people? Or do you want God's honor—the giving of life, the sacrifice of service?

If it's God's honor, then, surprise you though it may, that has to be earned. Jesus said, "If any man serve me, him will my Father honour" (John 12:26). Romans 2:7 declares "by patient continuance in well-doing seek for glory and honour." Romans 2:10 says, " . . . honour . . . to every man that worketh good." You see, the honor is according to the good. The greater the work, the greater the honor.

Only that work done in God's power for God's glory will be honored.

But in a great house there are not only vessels of gold and of silver, but also of wood and of earth; and some to honour, and some to dishonour. If a man therefore purge himself from these, he shall be a vessel unto honour sanctified, and meet for the master's use, and prepared unto every good work (2 Tim. 2:20-21).

The choice, then, is to be either a clay pot, tucked away on some dusty self, or to be fine china displayed by the Master on the most special occasions. To receive a better understanding of this principle, let's examine a parallel passage, 1 Corinthians 3:11-15.

For no other foundation can anyone lay than that which is laid, which is Jesus Christ. Now if any one builds on the foundation with gold, silver, precious stones, wood, hay, stubble—each man's work will become manifest; for the Day will disclose it, because it will be revealed with fire, and the fire will test what sort of work each one has done. If the work which any man has built on the foundation survives, he will receive a reward. If any man's work is burned up, he will suffer loss, though he himself will be saved, but only as through fire (RSV).

What does this passage teach? First, our acceptance before God is founded on Jesus Christ. There's no other way, no other foundation except him. Once this foundation is beneath us, we can then get on with building our lives. There are two kinds of material with which to build: Gold, silver, and precious stones or wood, hay, and stubble. What's the difference? Wood, hay, and stubble are combustible materials; but gold, silver, and precious stones aren't (Num. 31:23).

You can build with any or all, and no other person may know what you're made of. But on that last day, it'll be revealed. Those Christians who attempted good works in their own power, in their own natural capacities (wood, hay, stubble), will see their works rejected and burned. They'll still go to heaven because they built on the right foundation (Jesus Christ), but, having built with the wrong material (wood, hay, stubble), they'll not be rewarded like they thought. However, those Christians producing a goodness not of this earth (gold, silver, precious stones) will have their goodness rewarded. Build with the right materials, Christian. The only work that will be honored is the work performed in God's power, for God's glory.

There's a blessing and a challenge in this message. The blessing is that God has crowned us with honor—in God's eyes each person is special. The challenge is that we need to seek the right honor (not the honor of others, not the honor of self, but the honor of God) in the right manner (not in your might, but in his, not for your glory, but for his). Then we need to honor one another—take the initiative, look for opportunities to bless, and make those in the body know— "to me and to God, you're very special!"

9
Hospitality One to Another

The one-another statements are God's specific instructions on how we are to relate to believers in the body. Some worry that an emphasis on fellowship will divert from the important task of evangelism. But God has two ways of reaching the lost: (1) preaching ("How shall they believe in him of whom they have not heard? and how shall they hear without a preacher?" Rom. 10:14) and (2) fellowship ("That they also may be one in us: that the world may believe that thou hast sent me," John 17:21). Acts 2:46-47, John 13:34-35, and many other passages stress what most churches have forgotten: The lost are won not only by hearing the gospel (preaching) but also by seeing it (fellowship). I suspect the poet spoke the sentiment of many when he wrote: "I'd rather see a sermon than hear one."

Thus 1 Peter 4:9 exhorts: "Use hospitality one to another." Of all people, the Christian is have an open heart, an open hand, and an open door. Romans 12:13 says we're to be "given to hospitality." That is, we're to have a knack, a desire, and a budget for hospitality —cultivated, of course, by much practice. Titus 1:7-8 says ministers should be lovers of hospitality. Hospitality ought to occupy such a special place in our hearts that we look for opportunities to render it. But, what is hospitality? The South is supposed to be famous for it, but do we really know what biblical hospitality is? The Greek word for hospitable is *philoxenos*—*philos,* meaning brotherly love, and *xenos,* meaning a stranger. Literally, then, hospitality means a brotherly love toward strangers. But doesn't 1 Peter 4:9 have fellow believers in mind when it says "use hospitality one to another"? Yes, but keep in mind the church is filled with strangers who have known each other for years. What a contradiction to Christian fellowship! God wants his people loving one another past the superficial exchanges strangers give. Hospitality is more than the cordial gestures of Southern charm. Hospitality is an investment of quality time in which we're used of God to meet another's need.

Hospitality Usually Involved a House

The New Testament church met in houses. The Roman decree issued by Nero made it unlawful for believers to build a church. The first church building we know about wasn't erected until 265 AD in faraway Persia. The church—without temples, without cathedrals, without sanctuaries—experienced such remarkable growth that historians claimed the evangelization of the whole world was clearly in sight.

Then the church experienced a blessing which turned out to be a curse. By fiat Constantine declared the whole Roman Empire to be Christian. With that decree, Christians stopped meeting in houses and started meeting in sanctuaries. The church grew stronger as an institution, but weaker as a church. Historically this period is called the Dark Ages. Tragically, under institutionalism (which we still have today) the church lost a dimension which needs to be recovered. Believers need to recover an intimate sharing around the Word, where there's an enmeshing of lives in the power of the Spirit.

Since real hospitality has been covered up by a lot of Sunday pretense, where's the best place to uncover it? Biblically, historically, and practically, hospitality involves a home. Of course, hospitality may express itself outside of your house. But when you bring somebody into your home, your hospitality takes on an inclusiveness which God blesses in a special way.

The purpose of hospitality is to deepen relationships, to meet needs, to share in the sufficiency of Christ, and to rejoice in his creation. Hospitality may take the form of a meal, an evening discussion, a day at the beach, or a trip to the zoo. It may mean sharing the witness of the Word or spending a season in prayer. It may mean a bed, some clothes, some money, or even a shoulder to cry on. Always, though, hospitality means sharing *you*. And ultimately, hospitality means sharing *Jesus*. Hospitality is cultivating a relationship in order to share the riches of Christ.

With Whom Are We to Be Hospitable?

There's no formula to this, so I don't want to be too rigid. The principle is that every Christian is to give hospitality; but Christians gifted in hospitality are to invest themselves in a more sustained manner, in the more difficult situations. However, the Christian not gifted in the area of hospitality should have a growing edge. He should expand his hospitality to include those people who don't give an immediate, gratifying response. Very often this means a stranger and more often this means an unbeliever.

Since hospitality is closely linked with strangers, let's study what the Bible says about them. In the ancient Mediterranean world a stranger was considered an enemy. In fact, there was a hypnotic fear of strangers. If you happened to be a stranger in another land, you were inviting the worst kind of abuse—robbery, rape, assault, and maybe even death. Very frankly, there was little legal protection against such.

The people of Israel knew what it was to be strangers. They suffered one exile after another. By experience, they knew how vulnerable and abused strangers were. Because of these experiences and because of the message God gave them, Israel introduced a new attitude toward strangers, an attitude of hospitality. In Exodus 22:21, God told his people, "Thou shalt neither vex a stranger." In Exodus 23:9, God said, "Thou shalt not oppress a stranger: for ye know the heart of a stranger, seeing ye were strangers in the land of Egypt." Jeremiah and Ezekiel stressed the same truth: No harm is to be done to the stranger. On the positive side, Deuteronomy 26:12 instructs God's people to give food and clothing to the stranger. Numbers 9:14 urges God's people to give legal protection. Second Chronicles 6:32 includes strangers in worship. Deuteronomy 10:19 sums it all up by saying, "Love ye therefore the stranger." Deuteronomy 10:18 notes that God "loveth the stranger." The psalmist declared, "The Lord preserveth the strangers" (146:9). No doubt about it, God is on the side of the stranger.

Who is the stranger? The stranger is the one who is different, the one who doesn't know anybody, the one just passing through. Away from home, away from family, away from friends, the stranger is understandably lonely, maybe even a little bit anxious. What an opportunity! God wants us to treat strangers like brothers and sisters in the Lord (3 John 5). We are to give the stranger a home away from home.

Of course, there must be caution. But don't hold out for a risk-free situation because you won't find it. Such a situation didn't exist in biblical days, and it doesn't exist today. Hospitality always involves risk—physical risk, property risk, ego risk, and spiritual risk. Are we willing to take those risks? Is hospitality a regular part of our ministry? How will we answer God on that last day when he asks us about our ministry of hospitality?

Hindrances to Hospitality

I think there are two major hindrances to the ministry of hospitality: the hindrance of time and the hindrance of motive. Actually, the two are related. If you don't want to be hospitable, you certainly won't find the time. So let's focus first on motive.

Do we want to open our homes and hearts to those people who need us? Do we want God to use us as we venture beyond self, family, and friends? Most of us probably don't have any enthusiasm for this ministry. That is because we're not especially excited about what God is doing in our lives. We need to go beyond the staleness of sin and self and let God use us in a new, uplifting way.

Jesus said, "He that gathereth not with me scattereth abroad" (Matt. 12:30). In other words, we're either gatherers or scatterers. Which are you? Do you have a healing influence? Do you draw people in? Do you make them feel welcome? Or do you repel people? Do you split them up? Do you bring about division?

I'm concerned that we have people today who are practicing hypocrisy in reverse. Hypocrisy is trying to pretend that you're more than you really are. But hypocrisy in reverse is pretending you're less than you really are. According to the Bible, Christians are ambassadors for God to a lost, dying world. If our lives don't convey that, we are practicing hypocrisy in reverse!

Why Hospitality?

First Peter 4 urges hospitality but not before dealing with the problem of motive. "Forasmuch then as Christ hath suffered for us in the flesh, arm ourselves likewise with the same mind."

Why should we reach out and give? The attitude of gratitude— that's why. Jesus reached out to us and it cost him plenty. We're not being sent as sheep to the slaughter. Yes there's suffering ahead, but the Bible says, "Arm yourselves." The Greek word is *oplisasthe,* indicating arming with the heaviest armor for maximum protection. The armor is the mind of Christ. Spiritual growth means nothing more, nothing less, than having Christ's mind. To have Christ's mind means we'll do what we naturally don't want to do—to be God's people to those who aren't grateful. Let's see how the mind of Christ works:

For he that hath suffered in the flesh hath ceased from sin; That he no longer should live the rest of his time in the flesh to the lusts of men, but to the will of God (1 Pet. 4:1-2).

So, to follow Christ means we're no longer under sin's control. We may still struggle, but sin isn't winning—Christ is! Are you on the front lines of Christian service so intent on following Christ that sin is left behind? How we spend our time—"in the flesh to the lusts of men" or "to the will of God"—says something about our Christian commitment. How does your calendar and clock testify of the lordship of Jesus? Paul's motto, "Redeeming the time" (Eph. 5:16; Col. 4:5), should become ours. Wake up! Soft Christianity is the laughing-stock of hell.

Don't turn down the ministry of hospitality with "I don't have time." Time is the only thing we do have. Here is one way to assess how you're spending your time. Write down all of the demands of your present schedule. List every investment of time. Divide your list into three categories: activities which are of the Lord, those which are not of the Lord, and those which you're not sure about. Project into your schedule certain tasks which God says every Christian should be performing, such as hospitality, evangelism, and discipling. As you pray and project, let this be your guiding principle: Say no to the lesser, yes to the greater. Be tough. In the words of Hebrews 12, "Lay aside every weight." Whatever keeps you from doing what God wants you to do, lay it aside, cast it off, put it down. That's what we must do if we're to be good stewards of time.

The rest of time . . . to the will of God. Is that the prayer of your heart? If so, you have the mind of Christ. One thinks about how Jesus engaged the woman of Samaria. It was high noon—the desert sun was hot. This woman, so looked down on by others, couldn't even draw water from the well when the other women did. So, wanting to avoid the hushed whispers and the catty remarks, she went to the well at the hottest time of day. There she met Jesus. He confronted her in her sin with great tenderness. He reached out, and she responded. In fact, what took place in the woman's heart was so real that she was able to overcome tremendous hostility, persuading hundreds to "come, see a man, which told me all things that ever I did: is not this the Christ?" (John 5:29). When the apostles returned with their provisions for the meal, Jesus said, "My meat is to do the will of him that sent me, and to finish his work" (v. 34).

Are we as faithful to God's will as we are to our hunger pains? The daily desire to eat is a part of our humanity; the daily desire to do his will is a part of our Christianity. Just as we experience discomfort, sometimes intense discomfort, when we miss a meal, so we'll experience discomfort, sometimes intense discomfort, when we miss God's will. Eating is an occasion for much pleasure. So is the fulfillment of God's will. However, it wasn't always this way with us.

For the time past of our life may suffice us to have wrought the will of the Gentiles, when we walked in lasciviousness, lusts, excess of wine, revellings, banquetings, and abominable idolatries (1 Pet. 4:3).

Pleasure was once our guiding principle. We did what we wanted to do. That's proof positive that we weren't Christian, but it's not that way anymore: "Wherein [now] they think it strange that ye run not with them to the same excess of riot, speaking evil of you" (1 Pet. 4:4).

The world is always surprised and sometimes offended by that one who doesn't go along. The Greek word for "run" means to run with the pack—a vivid word picture of those whooping it up and having a great time on their way to hell. The Scriptures say these "shall give account to him that is ready to judge the quick and the dead" (1 Pet. 4:5). In fact, "For this cause was the gospel preached also to them that are dead, that they might be judged according to men in the flesh, but live according to God in the spirit" (1 Pet. 4:6).

Not wanting anybody to quake at the judgment, God gave the gospel, his good news, so no one would go to hell but would learn instead how to live "according to God in the spirit. But the end of all things is at hand: be ye therefore sober, and watch unto prayer" (1 Pet. 4:7).

Verse 5 says God was ready to judge. Verse 7 says the end was near. But these words were written over nineteen hundred years ago. What do they mean today? In his second epistle, Peter taught that Jesus is delaying his coming in order to give people a chance to repent. Nonetheless, the end is still near, in that Christ is not far off; he is at hand, standing just outside the door, ready to reenter history and call it to a close.

However, whether Christ comes or we leave, we need to be sober and watch unto prayer. By "be sober," Peter wasn't chastising the drunk. It's possible, of course, to be "mentally drunk." People can be mentally drunk over sports, so caught up by what's happening in the game they become oblivious to everything else. They can be caught up with gardening or some other hobby. Drunkenness is conveyed by disorientation and unawareness. So in effect Peter was saying, Christian, be alert, know what's happening, exercise good judgment, tune in to reality, and get your priorities straight. "And above all things have fervent charity among yourselves: for charity shall cover the multitude of sins" (1 Pet. 4:8).

Notice the emphasis Peter gave, "above all things have fervent charity." The Greek word for "fervent" means "stretched out." Have you ever seen a runner about to cross the finish line? He stretches out, giving it all he's got. That's what we're to do. Instead of running with the pack going to hell, we're to run God's race with a stretched-out love for fellow believers. This love, Peter said, covers a multitude of sins. Not a "Watergate cover-up" but a capacity to overcome the foibles of frail, feeble Christians.

Peter also said, "Use hospitality one to another without grudging" (v. 9). It really cost something to be a Christian in Peter's day. Many were under persecution, fired from their jobs, disowned by their families, and thrown out of their houses. To these people who were uprooted without money and without companionship, Peter urged an ungrudging hospitality. Obviously hospitality has its inconveniences, but if we focus there we might as well quit. Nobody is going to be blessed if we keep reminding them in not too subtle ways about how much we've done for them. Remember, our motive must be gratitude; our attitude, the mind of Christ; our plan, to meet others' needs; and our goal, to bring them to Christ.

Jesus said:

When you give a luncheon or dinner, do not invite your friends, your brothers or relatives, or your rich neighbors; if you do, they may invite you back again so you will be repaid. But when you give a banquet, invite the poor, the crippled, the lame, the blind, and you will be blessed (Luke 14:12-14, NIV).

Loving friends is not wrong, but Jesus is calling us to something greater. Is there a lonely person you need to love? A single-parent family you could include in your entertainment? That's what hospitality is all about, going out of our inner circle to be a blessing to others.

The Rewards and Consequences

Hebrews 13:2 admonishes, "Be not forgetful to entertain strangers: for thereby some have entertained angels unawares." This verse, which uses the same word for *entertain* that Peter used for *hospitality*, probably refers to the time when Abraham was hospitable to three strangers, only to learn that one was God and the other two were angels. Extending ourselves in hospitality, opening our homes to strangers, may result in blessings so rich that you'll consider it (like the angels) to be the nearest thing to God. We need to be sensitive to the unblessed, love-starved people who cross our paths. God wants us to do what the natural part of us will never do—to be hospitable. Jesus made hospitality the criterion for judgment.

When the Son of man shall come in his glory, and all the holy angels with him, then shall he sit upon the throne of his glory: And before him shall be gathered all nations: and he shall separate them one from another, as a shepherd divideth his sheep from the goats: And he shall set the sheep on his right hand, but the goats on the left. Then shall the King say unto them on his right hand, Come, ye blessed of my Father, inherit the kingdom prepared for you from the foundation of the world: For I was an hungered, and ye gave me meat: I was thirsty, and ye gave me drink: I was a stranger, and ye took me in: Naked, and ye clothed me: I was sick, and ye visited me: I was in prison, and ye came unto me. Then shall the righteous answer him, saying, Lord, when saw we thee an hungered, and fed thee? or thirsty, and gave thee drink? When saw we thee a stranger, and took thee in? or naked, and clothed thee? Or when saw we thee sick, or in prison, and came unto thee? And the King shall answer and say unto them, Verily I say unto you, Inasmuch as ye have done it unto one of the least of these my brethren, ye have done it unto me. Then shall he say also unto them on the left hand, Depart from me, ye cursed, into everlasting fire, prepared for the devil and his angels: For I was an hungered, and ye gave me no meat: I was thirsty, and ye gave me no drink: I was a stranger, and ye took me not in: naked, and ye clothed me not: sick, and in prison, and ye visited me not. Then shall they also answer him, saying, Lord, when saw we thee an hungered, or athirst, or a stranger, or naked, or sick, or in prison, and did not minister unto thee? Then shall he answer them, saying, Verily I say unto you, Inasmuch as ye did it not to one of the least of these, ye did it not to me. And these shall go away into everlasting punishment: but the righteous into life eternal (Matt. 25:31-46).

Hospitality, or the lack of it, is the litmus test of love. To those people who prayed, studied their Bibles, and never missed a Sunday at church, *but* who never gave themselves to hospitality, God will say, "Depart from me; I never knew you." Be clear on this, hospitality isn't the basis of salvation; it's the result of it. So, won't you show your love for Jesus by making room in your heart and in your schedule for this all-important ministry, the ministry of hospitality?

10
Be Kind One to Another

Ephesians 4:32 urges, "Be ye kind one to another." Romans 12:10 says, "Be kindly affectioned one to another." Both teach God's desire for kindness. Admittedly, I come to this study on kindness with some hesitation. You see, nearly everybody is in favor of kindness.

The title of a popular song, "Try a Little Kindness," expresses the universal sentiment: We ought to be kind to one another. Most everybody believes that; you do, I do. There isn't a respectable religion or philosophy around that denies it. So why tell people what they already believe? Besides, what does Christianity have to say that differs from other perspectives. Is kindness really produced only by God's Spirit?

The Motive and Goal for Kindness

What Christianity teaches *is* different from what other perspectives teach. The reason most people are willing to be kind is because they believe that a person is worthwhile, that a person has value. So far, so good—Christianity agrees. But here's where we part company. The world believes that a person has value simply because of who he is. He is a person; therefore, he has intrinsic value.

Christianity says a person is valuable, not because of who he is but because of whom he could become. True, everybody has value because they were created by God, but this value is tentative. One day God will banish countless people whom he created and loved and, by leaving them in the outer darkness, he'll declare them utterly

99

worthless. Our value is determined by our relationship with God. If we reject him, we have no value. All that is good about us will fade when our lives becomes consistent with our rejection of God. But if we accept God, we'll have unmeasured value. Because you were created, you have some value. But it's not until you become a new creature, not until you invite Jesus to be the Lord of your life, that your life will take on an eternal value.

This is immensely important, for out of this truth we learn the *motive* for kindness and the *goal*. We're to be kind to others, not because of who they are but because of whom they could become. If we're not motivated in the right way, we won't be kind in the right way. In fact, we may not be kind at all. If we respond to people because of who they are, what happens if we don't like them for who they are? Does kindness end? It does for many people. If people are mean, spiteful, or obnoxious, others usually give up on them. If people are ungrateful, unlovable, and unresponsive, others frequently want nothing more to do with them. People who offer kindness from the wrong basis are often left without adequate motivation. And being without that, they pass up many, many opportunities to be kind.

The real motivation for kindness is found, I think, in Colossians 3:11-12: "Christ is all, and in all. Put on therefore . . . kindness."

Jesus Christ, the very presence of God, is in or near every human heart. Because of that fact, people have value; and this value, whether real or potential, provides tremendous motivation for being kind. You can say to yourself, "Christ is close to that person. So I'll be kind because Christ wants to live in him and make him new."

Having said this much, we can anticipate the right *goal* for kindness: to lead someone into a redemptive relationship with the Lord, a relationship that will give that person an eternal and an ever-increasing value. The world doesn't have this goal. What the world calls kindness is nothing more than a ministry to temporary, earthly needs—some food, some clothing, some money. These are the things the world gives in the name of kindness.

Of course, kindness includes seeing to physical needs, but it includes more. Kindness also provides for the soul. Kindness provides for the hereafter, not only here and now. Most importantly, kindness provides a Provider, not just some provisions. The scope of Christian kindness goes far beyond what the world means by kindness. Kindness isn't just an innocuous term, meaning "be polite; do a good deed." Kindness is a robust term, conveying by practical goodness a desire for the other person to come to know the Lord.

Components of Kindness

What is Christian kindness? Kindness is the Holy Spirit sharing you with people in need in such a way that those people are immeasurably blessed. Notice: the Holy Spirit shares *you*, not just your things. There's a kind of philanthropy that doles out its goods crassly and mechanically, but the giver never really touches the life of the one who receives. However, kindness involves relationship—one heart reaching out to another in the energy of the Holy Spirit.

The Scriptures indicate that kindness has several components. Hebrews 5:2 tells us that we're to be kind to the ignorant. So kindness is sensitive and patient. First Thessalonians 2:7 likens kindness to a nurse who loves her children. So kindness is tenderhearted and compassionate. Second Corinthians 6:6 links kindness to ministry. So kindness is generous. Second Peter 1:7 links kindness with godliness and love. Since godliness and love are two highest descriptions of God, for kindness to be sandwiched between them is an indication that kindness is one of the highest of all virtues.

A quick survey of related passages seems to indicate that kindness is often targeted for those who don't deserve it. For example, Nehemiah 9:17 links slowness of anger with kindness. Second Peter 1:6-7 relates patience and godliness to kindness. And a great many passages (Pss. 117:2; 119:76; Isa. 54:8; Col. 3:12) relate mercy to kindness. So, kindness is to be the response we make to those who hurt or offend us. Again, we must be absolutely clear on the motive and goal. If we are not clear on these two points, we won't be kind.

The Opposite of Kindness

Having some idea of what kindness is, what is the opposite of kindness? To get an answer to that, let's consider these words from Titus 3:2: "Speak evil of no one . . . avoid quarreling . . . be gentle . . . show perfect courtesy toward all men" (RSV). Speaking evil and quarreling is set against being gentle and courteous.

In the Scriptures, "gentleness" and "kindness" are nearly synonymous. In the Greek Old Testament and in other parts of the Scriptures, those words are virtually interchangeable. So, this verse is very much related to our discussion. The term *courteous* means more than mere politeness, more than routine adherence to social amenities.

The Revised Standard Version talks about "perfect courtesy"—in other words, a gracious disposition that goes all out to help somebody else. The King James Version uses the word "meekness"—meaning that the self is under control, allowing the outer expression of love to flow into the lives of others. On one side of the contrast, we have this gracious disposition that goes all out to love others. Now lets see what's on the other side.

"Speaking evil" refers to the mean, slanderous things that we say about other people. Rene Pascal, the famous French thinker, who probed not only the secrets of the universe but also the secrets of the human heart, said: "I set it down as a fact that if all men knew what each said of the other, there would not be four friends in the world." I hope that's not true, but it may be that it is. What we say about people, even those people we call our friends, is shameful. There is no telling how many people have been hurt by our cruel and thoughtless words. Jesus issued a very stern warning about such words—especially the venomous, deadly, hissed-in-hatred words we sometimes utter. "By your words you will be justified," Jesus said, and "by your words you will be condemned."

Now, in order to know what Jesus meant, maybe it would be helpful to recall the experience of former president, Richard Nixon. Richard Nixon might never have been forced out of office if it hadn't been for the tapes of conversations in the executive office. Those tapes—more than anything else—were responsible for his resignation.

Jesus would have us remember that our words are being stored up. Nothing we say escapes God's notice. We'll have to give an account. No wonder the Scriptures declare, "Speak evil of no one" (Titus 3:2, RSV). Such talk is completely contrary to God's kindness.

The Bible also tells us to "avoid quarreling" (Titus 3:2, RSV). Evil speaking occurs behind other people's backs, but quarreling is a face-to-face encounter. Quarreling involves one ego against the other, each out to win, each determined to get its own way. This determination to get our own way can become so intense that all restraints are broken. When this happens, there's very little we're not capable of. A murderous spirit may even sufrace. Each year people go to their graves because of some minor quarrel. Harsh words are said. A passion of hatred begins to grow and, before you know it, somebody has done an awful act that he never thought he could do.

Most everyone has experienced this swelling spirit of hatred. We don't like that about ourselves, but we know that there's within us a capacity to murder. One way to handle this is to follow the Scriptures' advice to "avoid quarreling." Someone has said that the best way to defeat the demon of quarreling is to starve it to death. In other words, refuse to fight. Avoid quarreling.

Speaking evil and quarreling are the opposites of kindness. Speaking evil and quarreling represent attempts to bring a person down, to hurt him and, sometimes, to do physical harm. Kindness is motivated to give a person a lift by being good and loving.

The Counterfeits of Kindness

Satan will conterfeit God's work any way he can. He counterfeits so he can cause us to accept far less than what God intends to give. How does he do that with kindness? Several ways, one of which we've already mentioned. Satan will lead people to think about kindness only in terms of material giving. As a result, Christians will give less and the people God wants to reach will receive less. A hungry person can fill up on an exquisite meal or, if need be, junk. Either will take hunger away. Thus, we need to be sure that what we're offering is God's best.

Our kindness must go beyond what the world can give. Anybody can offer a cup of water. But Christians are to offer a cup of water *in His name*. We minister to only a part of a person when we give the cup of water, and that satisfaction is only temporary. However, Christian kindness ministers to the whole person, making sure that person is blessed with an eternal satisfaction. Do you see the difference?

Another way Satan counterfeits kindness is by oozing lovey-dovey concern just so he can manipulate and draw us offsides. He did this to Jesus in the wilderness. Satan knew that Jesus hadn't eaten for forty days. Satan came to Jesus, sounding humane and kind, "Jesus, you're hungry," he said. "I hate to see you hungry like this. Why don't you turn the stones into bread? You can do it. Go ahead and eat." In his shrewd and crafty manner, Satan was tempting Jesus to forsake not only the guardianship of the Father but also his identity with humanity. The Bible calls Satan "an angel of light." And no wonder! Sometimes he's so attractive, so compelling! He appears to be kind, gracious, and loving. But beware! The design and purpose of what he's doing is straight out of hell.

How to Be Kind

We've talked about what kindness is, what it isn't, and how it may be counterfeited. We even know why we should be kind. Now how do we do it? First Samuel 20:14 says kindness is "of the Lord," Second Corinthians 10:1 says kindness (gentleness) is "of Christ," Galatians 5:22 says kindness (gentleness) is of the Holy Spirit. So the Triune God is the true source of kindness, but how do we become kind?

Romans 2:4 says: "Do you not know that God's kindness is meant to lead you to repentance?" (RSV). We've been blessed so many times we now take blessings for granted. God sends earthly blessings as an inducement for his heavenly blessings. God is good.

He wants to bless us with salvation.

Paul made this clear in his letter to Titus.

For we ourselves also were sometimes foolish, disobedient, deceived, serving divers lusts and pleasures, living in malice and envy, hateful, and hating one another. But after that the kindness and love of God our Saviour toward man appeared, not by works of righteousness which we have done, but according to his mercy he saved us, by the washing of regeneration, and renewing of the Holy Ghost; which he shed on us abundantly through Jesus Christ our Saviour (Titus 3:3-6).

For a long time we were anything but kind. Nonetheless, God was kind to us. What was this kindness? "He saved us." The highest expression of kindness is God's salvation. But God doesn't offer salvation to us because of who we are. This passage profiles us as being totally unworthy. "Not by works of righteousness which we have done, but to his own mercy." We don't deserve God's kindness, and there's nothing we can do to deserve it. All we can do is receive God's kindness. But this is hard for us to believe because we've learned to become very cautious about any displays of kindness. We want to know why it's coming our way. What's in it for the person doing it? It's hard to believe God is kind just because he's kind! He gives us earthly kindnesses—food, clothes, shelter—the necessities of life, and sometimes, many luxuries. He gives us these for one all-important reason: We are his creation, made in his image and likeness.

God's heavenly kindness calls us to salvation, and our repentance must be real. That's the one condition for God's heavenly kindness—a true and sincere repentance. In the words of Joel, "Rend your heart, and not your garments" (2:13). Rending the garment was an Oriental expression of sorrow. But God doesn't want us just to go through the motions—walk the aisle, join the church, and pretend to begin a new life. God wants a repentance from the depths of our hearts. "Rend your heart and not your garments, and turn unto the Lord your God: for he is gracious and merciful, and . . . of great kindness."

God will give us the highest expression of his kindness, salvation, if deep down we repent of our sin and turn to him. God just wants to be kind to you! In his Word, he says:

With everlasting kindness will I have mercy on thee. . . . The mountains shall one day depart, and the hills be removed; but my kindness shall not depart from thee (Isa. 54:8,10).

We may be able to be kind in the ways that the world is kind, but we'll never be kind in God's way until we first receive his kindness. The principle is simple: You can't give what you don't have.

Is that it? Just "get saved" and you can be kind? Although salvation is the most important part of kindness, it is not all. There's a daily, ongoing dimension to receiving salvation. Even though we're members of God's family, much in our lives still need to be brought under the lordship of Jesus. The principle, then, is this: The more you receive God's heavenly kindness—salvation—the greater is your capacity to be kind to others.

There is one other principle that I want to share with you. James 3:17 says, "But the wisdom that is from above . . . is gentle." The word *gentle* and the word *kind* are synonymous. This verse could very well read, "But the wisdom that is from above is kind." This means that perspective we have is the most critical factor in whether we are going to be kind. If, in a moment of irritation, we focus on what somebody has done and what a no-good person that individual is, the natural self in us will lash out in retaliation. So when such temptations come, pray for the wisdom that is from above. Ask God to enlarge perspective, to change focus, to see things as he sees them. That way you'll be able to see why this person has offended you and, more importantly, how you can administer God's kindness.

"If any of you lack wisdom," Scripture says, "let him ask of God . . . and it shall be given" (Jas. 1:5). There's absolutely no reason for us to be mean because upon request we can have God's wisdom. And, in turn, God's wisdom will give us a perspective that'll motivate us to be kind.

If someone has treated you poorly, perhaps he was acting out of his own hurt. God's wisdom will help you focus not only on the other person's hurt but also on a way to heal it. Perhaps his treatment of you was completely uncalled-for. God's wisdom will help you realize that there have been times when you've done the same thing to God. Yet God remained kind to you. So shouldn't you, in this instance, be God's person and be kind to the person who doesn't deserve it?

The natural perspective is small, and it'll have us acting small. The wisdom which comes from above is great, and it will have us being kind.

Do you remember Stephen, the first Christian martyr? While his enemies hurled rocks at him, Stephen, the Scriptures say, "looked up stedfastly." Had Stephen focused on his enemies he would have died a bitter, angry man. But instead Stephen looked up stedfastly into heaven. Instead of the bitterness we might expect, Stephen died praying for the men who murdered him, asking God that they be forgiven. Such kindness!

Notice, though, the Bible says Stephen "looked up stedfastly." Sometimes we'll be tempted to be unkind. A quick glance upward, a faint request for God's wisdom, will never avert our desire to be mean. So what must we do? Look up stedfastly. Pray for wisdom fervently. Then and only then will we have the capacity to be kind. Kindness is a part of the character of God. And it can be a part of our characters too if God is in control of our lives.

Are you able to be kind even when things are going badly and you don't feel like it? Are you able to be kind when everything is going great and contentment restricts your vision about what the world is really like? You are if God is in control. Ask God to remain in charge of your life. Ask him to give you his wisdom, his perspective. Then, in season or out, try a little kindness.

11
Love One Another

The story is told of a Catholic priest who was assigned to a new parish. Wanting to know what his people were really like he decided to come to the village early. So, dressing as a beggar, lingering among the marketplace, and never letting on who he really was, he studied his people as they transacted their day-to-day business.

One day he found himself talking to a prim, proper, and fastidious lady, well schooled in the truths of the Bible. Quite naturally, the conversation turned to religion. "How many commandments are there?" the lady asked in a rapid-fire quiz designed to prove his ignorance. "Eleven," the beggar replied. "Eleven!," she repeated back, horrified at such ignorance. "Why, you know nothing of religion at all! Be gone, beggar man! Why should I spend my time with such as you?"

You can imagine the look on that lady's face when she came to church the following Sunday, only to discover the beggar was her new priest. What really stunned her, though, was the sermon he preached, entitled, "The Eleventh Commandment." His text came from Jesus' famous words in the upper room. "A new commandment I give unto you, That ye love one another; as I have loved you, that ye also love one another. By this shall all men know that ye are my disciples, if ye have love one to another" (John 13:34-35).

Actually, this commandment is given many times in the Bible. First Thessalonians 4:9, John 15:12, and Romans 13:8 all say "love one another." First Thessalonians 3:12 gives further emphasis, "Abound in love one toward another." And Romans 12:10 teaches,

"Be kindly affectioned one to another with brotherly love." The very badge of Christianity is love for fellow believers.

Jesus stood before a crowd one day and said, "Who is my mother? Who is my brother?" Then he answered his own question: "Whosoever shall do the will of my Father which is in heaven" (Matt. 12:50). Many, I suspect, know the reality Jesus was talking about. Some people are closer to other Christians than they are to some family members. Why? Perhaps some family members aren't Christian, or if they are, maybe they haven't grown in the faith very much. The result is that sometimes sharing with the church family is more fulfilling than sharing with the biological family. It doesn't have to be like this, but very often it is. Spiritual kinship can be stronger and dearer than flesh-and-blood kinship.

Strong spiritual kinship impressed the pagan world. To me, a successful ministry means that the world will be so impressed with the church's genuine and contagious love that they will want to be a part of the church. Whenever we talk about love, mush and piety have a way of propelling us into the unreal world of Never-Never Land. So, wanting to avoid that, let's simply and practically identify the kind of love the Bible talks about.

The Do's and Don'ts of Love

The love chapter of the Bible, 1 Corinthians 13, beautifully describes what love does do and what it doesn't do. Notice that nowhere in this chapter is love linked to feeling. Regrettably, many today see love as feeling. If smitten with ecstatic rapture, they'll love. And if not, they won't.

But nowhere does the Bible link love with feeling. That's because love isn't dependent upon feeling—it's dependent upon will. Quite simply, love is to will another's good. You may not feel like loving, but in God's power you can do it anyway. Let's look at the do's and don'ts of Christian love.

Charity suffereth long, and is kind; charity envieth not; charity vaunteth not itself, is not puffed up, doth not behave itself unseemly, seeketh not her own, is not easily provoked, thinketh no evil; rejoiceth not in iniquity, but rejoiceth in the truth; beareth all things, believeth all things, hopeth all things, endureth all things (1 Cor. 13:4-7).

This passage begins with a positive statement, lists several negative statements, and then concludes with some more positive statements. Let's look at each statement in turn. First, love "suffereth long and is kind."

By "suffereth long," the Scriptures simply mean patient. Actually, there are two forms of patience. The active form, "patient continuance" (Rom. 2:7)—meaning endurance, faithfulness and stedfastness. And the passive form, "patient waiting" (2 Thess. 3:5)—waiting, sometimes to the fourth watch (Mark 6:48) for God to make his move. True love both waits and endures. It waits for God to act and it endures the flaws and frailties of the old Adam until God acts. Paul quickly added that love is kind. It isn't on the sidelines, enjoying the luxury of a spectator's role. Love means being a channel of blessing to imperfect, and sometimes impossible, people. Love waits on God—knowing that different people have different timetables. It endures to the end—knowing that grace can change even the most obstinate sinner. Love is always kind—knowing that God's goodness can be mediated through a friend.

Now look at the negative statements. Love "envieth not" or more correctly, love doesn't become jealous. Notice that all the negative statements have one factor in common. They all involve an intrusion of self. Jealousy means wanting what another person has, wanting it so much that discontent broods within. This wanting isn't stimulated by the just object desired but by a desire to adorn self. The mentality being: If I just get such and such, the spotlight will be on me. Almost by definition, the person with envy is so cramped by his own discontent that he isn't willing to be a blessing to anybody.

Next we learn that love "vaunteth not itself, is not puffed up." Jealousy keeps a low profile. It's frequently a quiet, subtle, behind-the-scenes sin. But here the natural self grabs for glory, its real motives coming to light. Why, if no one else will do it, this bloated egotism will heap praise on itself. Have you ever known someone who was always fishing for a compliment, always having to be the center of attention, always concerned about how other people were taking him? Obviously, people like that have too many unmet needs.

Paul went on to write, love "doth not behave itself unseemly." The Greek word for "unseemly" literally means "without form." What this verse speaks to is a disgraceful behavior which violates all forms of decency. Watch it! When the bloated ego doesn't get its way, it attacks! Untold abuse is targeted against the person or party frustrating the demands of the ego.

Paul explained that love "seeketh not her own." When a person's only desire is to please self, he neglects the needs of others. His behavior is like a baby's. Babies don't think about caring for other people's needs. When babies don't get their way, they may wail away in red-faced anger.

Paul also said that love "is not easily provoked." This means that love isn't touchy. Love isn't thin-skinned. Love isn't set off in anger over the least little thing. I am very much alarmed at how many fragile egos we have in Christendom—egos seething in festering anger over the silliest little things. Shouting and pouting are poor advertisements to the faith because such actions do not reflect Christian grace.

Paul contended that love "thinketh no evil." By that, he didn't mean we're to be naive; armed with God's revelation, the Christian should be the one person who knows the score. What Paul was discouraging is the penchant of some always to think the worst. People who have negative feelings toward people, who prefer to think the worst, are in violation of these words and need to repent.

The Bible says that love "rejoiceth not in iniquity." Love may see the iniquity, but it won't rejoice in it. I'm afraid most of us, however, secretly relish the downfall of another. How eager we are to believe the worst scandals, especially of those who once walked with the Lord. We should grieve when a Christian is overcome with a fault! Satan can be fierce against those who are diligent in the Lord's work. Sure, he may not bother you that much because he may have you satisfied with do-nothing Christianity. But if *you* were on the front lines, could *you* withstand the attack? Perhaps not. So don't criticize. Remember, were it not for the Lord's protecting powers, we would all be sifted as wheat.

"Rejoiceth not in iniquity," the Word indicates, "but rejoiceth in the truth." Sometimes the truth focuses on iniquity. So how can we rejoice not in iniquity but rejoice in truth? We can rejoice because no matter how heinous the sin, transforming grace is always available. Grace can turn around an Eldridge Cleaver, a Charles Colson, a John Newton, and countless others who have sinned against the Light. The truth not only clearly perceives the perversity of human nature *but* it also perceives a way out—through God's redeeming, transforming grace!

Of course, the way out involves you. Love "beareth all things." Whatever the sin, whatever the suffering, love shoulders the burden and brings it to God. Burden-bearing means that we'll avail ourselves to others in sharing our inner lives. We'll team up together against sin, Satan, and self. In my mind, this burden-bearing ministry is love's highest work; it is doing what God wants most: conforming a believer to the image of God. Colossians 2:2 declares that we're to be "knit together in love." How comforting it is to have fellow believers committed to the solutions of your problems.

Love not only bears but it also believes. We have all seen people who love to wallow in their misery. They hug each problem so tight that one wonders if they really want a solution. Well, godly love isn't a soap-operaish sharing of problems. Godly love is out to find solutions. And once it finds them, it is determined to see those solutions put into place. Love is not just a burst of emotion. Love is practical, constructive, and intent on changing the inner person.

Next, we're told that love "hopeth all things." At this point love and faith unite. Love seeks the best. When love finds the best, faith prays that the best will take root and grow. What liberating power there is in the team ministry of faith, hope, and love! Can you imagine what it would be like to have another person seeking your best and then, having found it, lifting prayers on your behalf so you could receive it? That's what love does.

And then, of course, love "endureth all things." Amazing! *All* things! How much does our love endure? We may be a little embarrassed on that last day when we have to acknowledge just how little it took to terminate our love? Why, in some instances our love didn't endure *anything*! Jesus said, "The love of many shall wax cold" (Matt. 24:12). If we'll continue in Jesus' love (John 15:9), our love will become more like his—an "everlasting love" (Jer. 31:3) which never gives up.

Oh, there's so much else to be said about love—how it casts out fear (1 John 4:18), how it covers sins (Prov. 10:12), and how it constrains us from doing what we might otherwise do (2 Cor. 5:14), how it is comforting (Phil. 2:1), strong (Song of Sol. 8:6), and unquenchable (Song of Sol. 8:7). But the fact is that the love of God passes all knowledge (Eph. 3:19). We simply can't define it. But it can define us if we'll surrender to its powers and let it do its good work.

"By this shall all men know that ye are my disciples," Jesus said, "if ye have love one to another" (John 13:35). Jesus wants us defined and identified by love. Read what your Bible teaches about love, particularly this passage in 1 Corinthians 13. Notice the negative and positive statements about love. Sometime we may easily say that we do not do the things love should not do. But, sadly enough, we're not doing the constructive things we should do. Reexamine what the Bible has to say about love and prayerfully resolve to do exactly what love would have you do in each relationship, in each circumstance. Remember, according to the Bible, if you don't love God's children in the way God defines love, then you don't love God (1 John 4:20-21; 5:2). That's a sobering thought.

"My little children, let us not love in word, neither in tongue; but in deed and in truth" (1 John 3:18). In other words, don't just talk love, do it! Do it in truth (Eph. 4:15). Do it as God tells you. But, for goodness' sake, do it!

How to Love

But what if I'm not that loving of a person? How am I supposed to love? Well, if you're not that loving of a person, then instead of focusing on how you should give love, you should first focus on how you are going to receive it. First John 4:19 says, "We love him because he first loved us." When we receive God's love, that love has within it a capacity to return love. To be loving people, we must allow God to love us. The principle is simple: The more we receive, the greater our capacity to share.

How do you love the person you don't even like? The Bible says, "Let love be without dissimulation" (Rom. 12:9). Clearly, we're not to fake love. How, then, are we to love that person?

First, love that person, not because of who he is, but because of whom he can become. Remember, he is redeemable: God's image, however broken and shattered, is still in him. This is where believing and hoping come in. Look for the image of God and love that.

Second, love that person, remembering how God loved you when you were such an exasperation to him. If God could bear with you, and if you now have God's love to share, you know firsthand how love can endure.

Third, love that person from God's resources made available supernaturally to you through the Holy Spirit. Loving the unlovable is an act of faith. By faith, you trust God for the love you need. By faith, you trust God to transform not only this person but also your feelings and attitudes toward him.

I want to suggest some specifics on how we are to love others. Jesus said, "love one another, as I have loved you" (John 15:12). Obviously, if we want to know how to love others, we must understand how Jesus loved the apostles.

In the first place, he prayed for them. He stayed up all night trying to understand the Father's will. That means we're not to be too casual or too unreflective in our relationships. We're to make each relationship a matter of prayer. Have you done that? Have you prayed to God for guidance in the selection of your friends? Jesus did. Pray that God will help you to be his person in each relationship.

I don't think we can talk about praying for people without also mentioning our need to *believe* in people. By that, I mean that we need to believe in God's capacity to change them.

Peter Marshall had a sermon in which he imagined the kind of dialogue that would have taken place had each of the twelve been compelled to appear before a senate committee for approval to the high office of apostle. The city was filled with learned rabbis and dedicated priests. Whatever did Jesus mean by choosing a tax collector and a bunch of rowdy fishermen?

But Jesus believed in people. He had a great hope for these men, even when their behavior gave him little basis for it. One of the kindest and one of the most powerful things we can do is to hope for someone and believe in someone. Our hope and belief can give them the courage they need to become what God really wants them to become. God has encouraged us with just such a belief, but when it comes to other people, we give up rather easily. When God does do something wonderful in another person's life we, of all people, seem so surprised!

A third thing we can do for those God has given us to love is to "model the faith." By modeling the faith, I mean a quality investment of time where one takes another under his wing, systematically teaching him by word and deed how to apply the Scriptures to day-to-day life. Many Christians have not been impressed with this obligation. They may even think it egotistical to encourage someone to follow them. But that's how Jesus loved the apostles. Why did Jesus appoint the twelve? So they might take a course from him? So they might come to hear him preach? So they might watch him heal people? No. He appointed the twelve that they "might be with him" (Mark 3:14), that they might share his life. Those apostles watched morning, noon, and night as Jesus both fellowshipped and ministered.

Modeling means that we fellowship and minister too. We may lead people not only into a deep and honest fellowship but also into a challenging, life-expanding ministry. Of course, like Jesus, we must be prepared to give a lot of quality time. We must walk with our friends in all areas of life, sharing and teaching what God has given us.

Just now you may be saying to yourself—*Well, Jesus did that, but I'm not supposed to. Who am I to ask someone to follow me?*

You're not just asking someone to follow you. You're asking someone to follow you *as you follow the Lord.* That's what Paul did. Paul said, "You ought to follow our example. We were not idle when we were with you" (2 Thess. 3:7, NIV). To the Philippians, Paul wrote "Those things which ye have both learned, and received, and heard, and seen in me, do: and the God of peace shall be with you" (4:9). In the same letter, Paul said, "Brethren, join in imitating me, and mark those who so live as you have an example in us" (3:17, RSV). In a letter to the Corinthians he wrote, "I urge you, then, be imitators of me" (1 Cor. 4:16, RSV). There are many other Scripture passages which encourage the same thing. To love in this manner means you'll become an example, investing yourself in the most intimate way, in helping others to see the path God wants them to follow.

Fourth, as I think about how Jesus loved his apostles, it seems to me that he was not just a giver; he was also a receiver. Jesus willingly accepted help from other people—from the woman at the well, from Mary and Martha, from the apostles—especially from the apostles! Jesus poured his heart out to these men, inviting each to minister to him, to serve with him, and to pray for him. This is so important. If you really want to love someone, quit being so all sufficient; stop projecting the image of a complete and finished person.

Why? First of all, because it's a lie. None of us are as far along as we want others to believe. Whether we acknowledge it or not, we need people. We are dependent on others. The book of Ephesians mentions the riches of our inheritance in the saints. Only within the community of God's people will we ever discover how rich we are. If we resist the intimacy of give-and-take sharing, we'll never discover many of God's riches. That's what Jesus meant when he told us to lay up for ourselves treasures in heaven. Invest in people.

As we give ourselves to others, we need to keep in mind that others will resist what we have if we resist or ignore what they have. Nobody feels very comfortable with a person who won't allow others to participate in his life. So don't get locked into the role of always being the giver, the minister, or the savior. That's much too limiting.

For us to be really effective, we must allow others to participate in our lives. Let others give to you, let them minister to you, and let them help you. If you'll do that, you'll see that you won't lose your place of ministry as you had supposed. To the contrary, many more people will come to you once the word is out. They'll get more than advice —they'll get a relationship.

How are we to love others? First, pray for them. After getting a mental picture of certain people and their situations, we need to ask God to make us channels of blessing. Second, believe in others. Encourage them to become what they can become through God's Word and power. Third, model the faith before other people, inviting them to follow us as we follow the Lord. Fourth, receive from others. Other people must be allowed to participate in our lives in real and significant ways.

"Love one another"—this is Christ's eleventh commandment. It represents the badge of Christianity. How we need to develop this love in the church! For this love is proof positive that the gospel really works and that God's kingdom way of life is, indeed, at hand.

DOING THE WORD

Chapter 1

1. With your group, discuss the following:

   Am I wearing a veil? What is it and why?

   Is accountability among believers an option?

   If not, what kind of accountability should it be?

   Do I want to be a part of a group that solves problems biblically?

   If an outsider could see all that was going on in my church, would he conclude that Jesus is the Messiah? (John 17:21)

2. With the assistance of your pastor, ask the Holy Spirit to select the people with whom he wants you to cultivate deeper relationships.

3. It is important that every class or group be led by someone who fits the description of Romans 15:14: "full of goodness, filled with all knowledge, able also to admonish." That is, by precept and example the leader knows how to conform character to the image of Christ. Caution: We run from what we need most! There are some real risks to meaningful sharing, but if we allow these risks to send us off in retreat, we are saying, that God's plan is unworkable. The sharing recommended here isn't a soap-operaish, say-what-you-feel, let-it-all-hang-out thera-peutic orgy. The Freudian game of archaeology (digging in the conscious and subconscious past) is unbiblical. The purpose of this sharing is to surface every thought, attitude, and behavior which is a part of the old life and then to reconstruct each

biblically, conforming the inner person "to the fulness of the stature of Christ."

Chapter 2

1. With your group, discuss the following:

     From personal experience, what does it feel like to be rejected? Once rejected, what were some of the defenses you used?

     Think about the people in your own inner circle. How did they get there—by prayer? Or by conforming to what you like?

     Do you have a sustained, redemptive relationship with someone who is poor? With someone of another race? With someone who is rigid in his religion?

     Have you ever "endured" a difficult relationship, finally having it transformed by the Lord?

     What Scripture passages have encouraged you as you sought to be God's person in a difficult relationship?

2. Within your heart, consider some people in your church who aren't in fellowship with anybody. Pray about them. See what God would have you to do.

3. We say salvation by grace, not works. But our operating principle for fellowship has been works, not grace. How can we turn this around?

Chapter 3

1. With your group, discuss the following:

     When it comes to conflict, how humble am I? how teachable? how patient? how loving?

     Is there a group of people with whom you regularly share your burdens? What kind of burdens do you share—inner self or outer self?

     Read Matthew 7:1-5 and Romans 15:14. Could God use

you in the spiritual surgery of restoring one overcome by sin?

2. As a project, take to heart 1 Corinthians 13:7 and see how many people you can "believe in." Share what you did and the results which followed.

Chapter 4

1. List Satan's devices—what does he do to gain a victory over you? Compare lists. You might want to read C. S. Lewis' book *Screwtape Letters*.

2. List the six pieces of God's armor (Eph. 6). What does each piece mean? Explain how to put them on.

3. Pray about how God could use you to minister to people presently outside the circle of your influence.

4. Share with your group how your ministry of care is going. Be sure to focus on how you have included others to help. Assess the effectiveness of your follow-up.

Chapter 5

1. With your class or with a group of friends, discuss the following:
     How long has it been since you mourned over a sin?
     What kind of comfort do you offer others?
     What was the last trial you endured? Did you receive God's comfort?
     Are you able to use the Scriptures in your efforts to give comfort?

2. Keep track of the frequency of opportunity to minister God's comfort. Chances are if there aren't many opportunities, your relationships aren't deep enough.

3. Memorize key passages of the Bible for certain recurring problems. For example, loneliness, bitterness, fear, the loss of a loved one, or the inability to cope.

Chapter 6

1. With your class or with a group of friends, discuss the following questions:

   You pretty well know yourself. Are you ever fainthearted, small souled?

   Do you endure a difficult situation by grit and backbone? Or do you depend on the counsel of the Word and the power of the Spirit?

   At what level do you doubt God?—His presence? His power? His motive? His faithfulness?

   When "discouraged because of the way," do you allow others to encourage you? Or do you keep your discouragement to yourself?

2. Record every reference in the Bible that has in common the words "in Christ," "in God," or "in Him." Beside each reference write in your own words how that verse combats an inferiority complex. You may want your Sunday School teacher to help you.

3. At the end of each day, write down the significant problems which are troubling you. Then, using the Bible, "gird up the loins of your mind." Ask some Christian friends to help you. At the end of a month, be prepared to share in written form what you said, what you thought, what you did, and then how you marshaled the resources of Scripture passages to encourage you.

Chapter 7

1. With your class or with a group of friends, discuss the following:

   Are you one of those people addicted to the attention of others?

   Do you get your sense of self-worth from how other people respond to you?

   Are you so on the front lines of kingdom warfare that you're

developing an intimate camaraderie with those who serve
with you?

Do other people voice appreciation for the way God is
working in your life?

2. For one week keep track of the levels of your communication
(rituals, pastimes, activity, withdrawal, and intimacy). Then put
percentages by each according to frequency. Share with your
class the lessons you learned from this.

3. As a personal exercise: Using your church membership roll,
identify those people against whom you have a conscious
emotional blockage. If it's your problem, confess it. If it's their's,
deal with it, but don't allow the relationship to drift.

Chapter 8

1. With your class or a group of friends, discuss the following:

Which honor are you really wanting? honor from self? from
others? or from God?

Do you give preference to fellow Christians? Keep a record
for one month. What did you do that a non-Christian
wouldn't do?

If there is a conflict with which you're presently involved, ask
God and ask your class to help you identify any strife or
vainglory in you.

2. List some biblical ways you can help others feel special.

3. Commit yourself to acting on these ways. Share progress
reports with your group.

4. Ask your group to help you reflect on the source and motive of
your ministry.

Chapter 9

1. With your class or a group of friends, discuss the following:

Are you excited about giving yourself to a ministry of
hospitality?

Are you thrilled about what God is doing in your life?

Are you a gatherer or a scatterer? Explain.

Are you guilty of "hypocrisy in reverse"?

Do you have time for hospitality? Do your clock and calendar testify of the lordship of Jesus?

How "stretched out" is your love?

2. Pray. Allow God to send a settled conviction about how you can give your home for a ministry of hospitality.

3. Find out what your church's policy is in regard to helping strangers in need. Find out what problems your church has encountered. See what it is you can do to help.

4. Block out a regular period of time when others can arm you for ministry. What Scripture passages would you use to arm them?

Chapter 10

1. With your class or a group of friends, discuss the following:

Are you kind only to people you like?

Is your kindness geared more to the inner person than the outer person?

Do you have a problem with your tongue? Are you quarrelsome? If so, which Scripture passages apply?

2. Share with your class the motivation struggle you are having to be kind. Then, by prayer and the Word, get God's wisdom and chart out a strategy to overcome what hinders you.

3. Commit yourself to leading someone to the Lord through kindness.

Chapter 11

1. With your class or a group of friends, discuss the following:

Are you a feeling-motivated person? Or a commandment-motivated person?

Check yourself out with the biblical criteria. Ask: how patient am I? How stedfast? How kind?

Does self dominate me? Do I envy? Do I crave the spotlight? Do I throw a tantrum if I don't get my way? Am I thin-skinned? Am I willing to believe the worst?

Have I given myself to a burden-bearing ministry? Do I shrink my impossibility list by believing in what God can do? Do I allow this belief to capture my heart and activate me for good? Do I, in God's power, stay in the relationship determined to see it redeemed?

2. Commit yourself to loving a person you don't like. Guided by the Word, empowered by the Spirit, with input from the group decide on strategy. Then, as events unfold, share progress reports with your group. It's probably best not to mention the person's name.

3. Ask God to give you a Timothy, someone God lends for whom you can model his love.

4. If you're not ready to take on this responsibility, ask God to give you a Paul, someone God lends to model the faith for you.

Notes

1. Bruce Larson, *Dare to Live Now* (Grand Rapids, Michigan: Zondervan, 1972), p.78.

2. Arthur Custance, *The Doorway Papers* as quoted in Ray Stedman, *Riches in Christ* (Waco: Word Books, 1976), p. 198.

3. Ray Stedman, *Body Life* (Glendale: Regal Books Division, Gospel Light, 1972), p. 23.